MVFOL

CHECKLIST

FOR A

PERFECT

CHRISTMAS

D0193679

ALSO BY JUDITH BLAHNIK:

Ruth and Skitch Henderson's Seasons in the Country (with Ruth and Skitch Henderson)

Ruth and Skitch Henderson's Christmas in the Country (with Ruth and Skitch Henderson)

Bread Alone (with Daniel Leader)

Mudhens and Mavericks (with Phillip Stephen Schulz)

Checklist

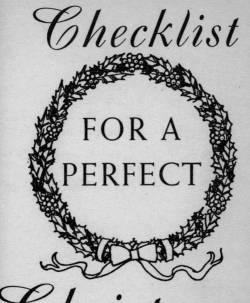

FOR A
PERFECT

Christmas

JUDITH BLAHNIK

MAIN STREET BOOKS
Doubleday
New York   London   Toronto   Sydney   Auckland

A MAIN STREET BOOK
PUBLISHED BY DOUBLEDAY
a division of Bantam Doubleday Dell Publishing Group, Inc.
1540 Broadway, New York, New York 10036

MAIN STREET BOOKS, DOUBLEDAY, and the portrayal of a building
with a tree are trademarks
of Doubleday, a division of Bantam Doubleday Dell Publishing
Group, Inc.

BOOK DESIGN BY CAROL MALCOLM RUSSO/SIGNET M DESIGN, INC.

Library of Congress Cataloging-in-Publication Data
Blahnik, Judith.
Checklist for a perfect Christmas / Judith Blahnik. — 1st ed.
p.   cm.
"A Main Street book"—T.p. verso.
1. Christmas—United States—Planning. 2. United States—
Social life and customs. I. Title.
GT4986.A1B53 1996
394.2'663—dc20   96-12956
CIP

ISBN 0-385-48221-3

Copyright © 1996 by Judith Blahnik
All Rights Reserved

PRINTED IN THE UNITED STATES OF AMERICA
OCTOBER 1996
FIRST EDITION

1 3 5 7 9 10 8 6 4 2

CONTENTS

Part I

CHRISTMAS PLANS AND CHECKLISTS

CHAPTER I
The Perfect Christmas

Contrary to popular belief, Christmas is not only for kids and families. Neither is it a holiday only for Christians despite the fact that it's the celebrated birthday of Christ; many of my agnostic friends are the most enthusiastic revelers I know.

Christmas is not even a single day, but a natural cycle that begins as the sun moves farther from the earth, the days shorten, leaves fall, and temperatures drop; it concludes as we celebrate, on Christmas Day, safe passage into the winter months. The whole cycle takes about eight weeks.

It's hard to appreciate Christmas as a natural event without understanding why we are drawn to celebrate winter. Long before the birth of Christ, people celebrated the Winter Solstice, the first day of winter, in much the same way as we celebrate Christmas—by making long-term preparations, then celebrating with song and music, prayers, and feasts that brought comfort and joy.

Solstice, which falls in mid-December, is the day that marks the beginning of winter. With only nine hours of light, it is the shortest day of the year. It made sense to celebrate the darkest day as a turning point in the seasons. Everything was bound to get better from that point on. The days would get longer and warmer with the gradual return of the sun and light; people could set their hopes on another spring; new life would come.

Fading days, lengthening nights, and hardening fields conspire to bring on an overwhelming sense of loss and wariness even if you've been through it before. Imagine what early humans must have felt as they watched the world grow so dark, without knowing for sure that the light would ever return or that life on earth would indeed continue. When I feel the anxiety of having only so many shopping days left, I imagine how it must have felt to think the world was about to collapse into total blackness, and it puts my problem into perspective.

The wonderful irony is that the fear of what is to come, and the burden of carrying that fear, has always been relieved by our preparations to meet it. Therein lies the attraction of making ready for and celebrating Christmas. The Christmas season is one of letting go of winter anxiety even though times feel scary; Christmas day is about finding out there is nothing to be afraid of—life and renewal is on the way.

WHAT IS THE PERFECT CHRISTMAS?

What is the perfect Christmas? Modern conventions give us an excellent outline that allows each of us to plan Christmas in a way that will guarantee a safe and joyous passage into the New Year.

We spend weeks preparing for a celebration that takes place in the home or gathering place of loved ones. There's a decorated tree, branch, or wreath to symbolize

hope and new growth; candles and lights to symbolize
the ability to confront darkness and anticipate the return
of light; greeting cards and shared food; and pledges or
toasts of love and caring. There are gifts to make us feel
more generous and warm when we give, and delighted
when we receive. And there are religious ceremonies,
carols, and processions to commemorate the life-affirming
relationship among God, earth, and people.

The perfect Christmas, however, does not require all
these familiar customs and trimmings, nor does it need to
mimic the one Charles Dickens popularized: warm polished oak mantels and balustrades laden with fresh greenery and candles, tables set with crystal and fine china, and
aromas of roasting meats and baked pies wafting from the
kitchen. The perfect Christmas is the one that you create
for yourself, drawing from your own memories, dreams,
and inclinations. It is a celebration that is uniquely
yours—with or without Santas on the roof or garlands on
the banisters, with or without chestnuts roasting and all
the conventions of Christmas perfectly in place.

This sounds simplistic, but so often people head full
speed into Christmas with checkbook or credit card wav-
ing, trying to re-create the ideal Christmas—a carbon
copy of scenes from movies, Currier and Ives or Norman
Rockwell paintings, or table settings from fancy food
magazines. By the end of the holiday they feel exhausted,
distracted, and untouched by what has happened, instead
of changed and hopeful.

The perfect Christmas is like a well-made play; the
structure is fairly standard, but the content and substance
is full of character and plot that is drawn from the deepest

and most personal part of your life—your own memory and dreams. If you have never sat down to think about what memories you can use in order to dream your plan for Christmas, now is the time to do it.

Charles Dickens once wrote: "My thoughts are drawn back, by a fascination which I do not care to resist, to my own childhood. I begin to consider what do we all remember best upon the branches of the Christmas Tree of our own young Christmas days, by which we climbed to real life."

Following a checklist, even *Checklist for a Perfect Christmas*, will not bring your holiday to life. Before planning the event, or even thinking about an organizational checklist, search out and claim what for you is at the heart of Christmas. That heart, whatever it is, lies in memory and upon the branches of your own young Christmases.

HONORING MEMORIES AND CREATING TRADITIONS

No matter who you are—a newlywed, an older-wed, a mom or dad, a single person living alone or with your significant other, or a member of a nontraditional family with two single adults and children—promise yourself you'll sit quietly for at least fifteen minutes and dream about Christmas past. Have a notebook close by. It's best to do this sometime in late October, before anyone has approached you about the holidays.

Memories

Close your eyes and allow memories of your own past Christmases to play before you, like a camera passing in slow motion over faces and rooms; outdoors, indoors, day and night.

Linger on the memories that made one particular Christmas or even just a moment at one Christmas a positive and spirited experience. Perhaps, when you were a child, a visiting relative gave you a new book and read to you on Christmas night. Stay with that memory until you can feel the quiet reassuring love and the pleasure of being read to. Write it down.

Then go back to collect more memories. Stay with each memory long enough to understand what about it still has meaning for you. Then write down a description of your memory in your notebook. Continue to do this until you have a list of important memories: the moment of mailing the letter to Santa; learning all the words to "The First Noel"; the smell of a favorite aunt's perfume; hearing the applause after your appearance in the school play; lighting the candle of the Advent wreath; searching for the perfect tree, cutting it, buying it, strapping it to the car, and enjoying its fragrance all the way home; leaving a note for Santa and actually finding it gone in the morning; feeling the leap in your heart on Christmas morning when presents that weren't there when you went to bed appeared miraculously under the tree.

The Plan

Now you have a list of positive memories. If other people in your life, kids included, have done this exercise, you

will find that you have *lots* of memories to work with.
Here are some examples:

- The pleasure of being read to
- Decorating cookies and packaging them up for gifts
- Sledding in the snow
- Putting the tinsel on the tree
- Singing with friends in the school choir
- Paints and picture books
- Warm socks
- Watching *It's a Wonderful Life*
- Midnight mass and choir procession on Christmas
  Eve
- Caroling at the rest home with friends
- A special Christmas Eve dinner
- Neighbors coming over the day after
- Horseback riding in the snow
- Playing basketball in the deserted schoolyard
- Getting to keep the wishbone
- Snowball fights with cousins
- Taking toys to the kids at the hospital

Let your memories guide you in making plans. You may
not make an exact re-creation of Christmases past, but the
joy of the memories will help shape your plans for the
holidays. For example, you might not have time to bake
and decorate cookies with your children; even so, you and
the children can go to a church bake sale, select cookies,
and pack some into colorful tins for friends; maybe you
do have time for one gingerbread house project; or perhaps this is the year your mother would like to visit and

bake cookies with the kids. Right there are three ideas to consider: Pick one and plan it into your holiday.

Perhaps it was always your job to put the angel on the tree because you were the oldest, youngest, whatever; do you want to pass on that tradition?

If they are consciously honored, all these positive reflections from the past can bring heart and energy to your Christmas plans, help them take shape, and make them shimmer with excitement and hope.

Do this exercise each year. Memories of recent Christmases can transform each new celebration. Who knows—a memory of a family bike ride can lead to a Christmastime train trek through the Canadian Rockies.

It's time to let your memories breathe and glisten again. Hang them on the branches of your new tree.

CHAPTER II
The Family Christmas

In every family I know, my own included, one person has acquired the role of producer/director of Christmas. Each year this person is the one to start the discussions, plan entertaining, initiate family communication, keep the calendar of social events, remember where the decorations are stored, plan the tree hunt, plan one or two special projects with the kids, delegate duties and responsibilities, and negotiate compromises. It's a big job. Even though some of us balk at the planning discussions that come up around the first of November, we do try to cooperate with this person.

AWAKENING THE SPIRIT

If you are the person who wears the Christmas producer/director hat in your family, then you are the one who must invoke the Christmas spirit. First, during a family gathering or through individual chats, simply talk about Christmas. Do this sometime in October, so the other people don't feel time pressures. Ask everybody, especially older family members, about their most vivid memories of past Christmases.

Most people will enjoy this brainstorming because you aren't necessarily pushing for any results other than the joy of remembering. Write down what everybody says in your Christmas notebook; be sure to add your own memories, as well. Then just let everything simmer for a while. This exercise begins to awaken the spirit of Christmas in family members and helps you to shape new events from old memories, creating a unique and fresh family Christmas.

Getting Started

In the first week of November, sit down with everyone and make an outline of all the ways to get ready for and have Christmas. Review the list of memories that you created, and ask for new ideas; this is the time when anyone who wants to try something new might bring it up. Ideas might include:

- Letters to Santa
- Cookies and gingerbread houses to bake and decorate
- Ornaments to make
- People to give cookies to—neighbors, friends, Grandma and Grandpa, teachers
- Parties for grown-ups and for kids
- Buying a tree

Let everyone tell you what comes to mind. Don't be a stickler for doing things the way they've always been done. If the kids are no longer interested in making Christmas cookies, that's okay. You can bake them for your own enjoyment. If somebody proposes to go skiing the day after Christmas, consider it. From all these propositions will come a real plan.

Checklist for a Family Christmas

It's time to move forward with your plans. Keeping a checklist is a great way to maintain momentum in your planning so that you don't get bogged down and forget things. Christmas is a before, during, and after holiday spanning eight weeks or so, and a checklist helps everybody in the family participate in the energetic flow of Christmas without feeling overwhelmed.

You may want to use the following checklist as is, or you may modify it to suit your own plans. Each item on the list pertains to only one thing so that you can keep focused.

November 1–7

☆ Decide where and how you'll spend Thanksgiving, Christmas, and New Year's. This may take a few discussions.

☆ If you are going to change a major tradition—for instance, the way you celebrate Christmas in the larger family—mention this to all concerned.

☆ If you will be traveling, make all hotel and car rental arrangements, confirm plane and train tickets, and so on. (See p. 46.)

☆   Decide on what in-home entertaining you will do. Include Thanksgiving in this discussion, too—how big an affair you want each event to be.

☆   Make a general list, in no particular order, of all the tasks you want to accomplish over the next eight weeks, including: decorating the home; hanging outdoor lights; buying the tree; sending Christmas cards; shopping for gifts, groceries, and miscellaneous items; making gifts (baking and crafts, wreaths); mailing packages; cleaning the house, doing any minor home repairs; attending school plays.

☆   Set a spending plan for the holidays, taking into consideration house decor, gifts, entertaining, special activities, travel, and the like.

☆   Make your gift lists. (Each person makes one.) (See p. 74.) Include homemade gifts such as cookies and jams (p. 103) and crafts such as candle holders, wreaths, and ornaments (p. 119).

☆   Plan to attend local craft fairs and cookie fairs for ideas.

☆   For fresh flower gifts, now is the time to start the bulbs for amaryllis and paperwhites. For dried flowers and herbs, now is the time to select hydrangeas for drying. Now is also the time to collect pinecones and branches for autumnal and winter decor.

☆   Collect baskets, tins, and containers for wrapping homemade gifts from the kitchen.

☆   Shop for and begin making craft gifts: ornaments, wreaths, and cards. (See p. 120.)

November 8–14
☆   Hang a special November/December calendar where all can see it and fill in set events: school plays, concerts, office parties, parents' nights out, the start of school vacation, parties in your home, when to expect relatives. Add your own deadlines for gift and meal shopping and home activities with the kids. Include tree-buying day.

☆   Plan your holiday parties, menu ideas, and guest lists. (See "Christmas Parties," p. 147.) Confirm invitations for Thanksgiving.

☆   Order your turkey for Thanksgiving.

☆   Make any special reservations for baby-sitters, car services, caterers.

☆   Stock up on tape, film, batteries, stamps, ribbon, wrapping paper, mailing boxes, tags, and envelopes.

☆   Continue making handmade ornaments and crafts that you want to give as gifts or keep for your own tree. (See p. 128.)

☆ Shop for gifts on your list. (See "Shopping Tips," p. 92.)

☆ Buy or make Christmas cards.

November 15–21
☆ Plan your Thanksgiving menu and shop for dry goods. If it's a potluck, let family and/or guests know what to bring.

☆ Start writing and addressing Christmas cards.

☆ Take out stored boxes of holiday ware—linen, china, and decorations. Try to inspect everything. Replace faded or broken items, buy fresh candles, glassware, and so on.

☆ Shop for gifts on your list.

☆ Cook some make-ahead meals for busy times coming up—two or three hearty soups and/or chilis and casseroles for suppers—and freeze them.

☆ Continue craft projects.

☆ Clean the house.

November 22–30

☆ If you haven't already done so, order gifts from catalogs. (See p. 95.)

☆ Decorate your house with autumnal branches, sprigs, corn swags, dried flowers, branches or autumn mums, a bowl of green apples.

☆ Buy the fresh groceries you need for Thanksgiving dinner, and enjoy the holiday. Make extra cranberry sauce for gift giving. (See p. 113.)

☆ Set aside a special Christmas corner, room, drawer, or closet. Make it handy for wrappings and gifts and decor.

☆ Complete your gift shopping.

☆ Start Christmas baking and freeze until ready for giving.

December 1–7

☆ Make an Advent wreath (see p. 140) and place it in a central location.

☆ Collect wish lists from the younger children. (See p. 79.)

☆ For the best selection, buy your tree now. (See p. 126.) Store it in a bucket of water in a cool place.

☆ Hang a wreath or swag on the door.

☆ Hang outdoor lights and decorations.

☆ Plan your holiday menus and assign potluck dishes, if any, to guests. (See p. 147.)

☆ If you plan to entertain, stock up on nonperishable supplies: wine, paper plates, and napkins.

☆ Complete Christmas baking and freeze—include gingerbread house or any ornament pieces. (See p. 135.)

☆ Complete any craft projects.

December 8–14

☆ Decorate the inside of your house with garlands, Christmas cards, and candles.

☆ If you haven't already done so, buy the tree. (See p. 126.)

☆ Wrap gifts for friends. Mail any that go out of town. (See pp. 99–101.)

☆ Take kids shopping for family presents. (See p. 94.)

☆ Cook and freeze make-ahead dishes for Christmas meals.

☆ Order special desserts or meats for Christmas dinner.

☆ Check Christmas wardrobe and take to the cleaner's, if necessary.

☆ Decorate cookies for ornaments or gifts. (Have the kids help.)

───────────────────────────────

December 15–21
☆ Organize Christmas music for your CD or tape player. (See p. 171.)

☆ Have a tree-trimming party for friends and family. (See p. 147.)

☆ Deliver gifts to neighbors and friends, teachers, and coworkers.

☆ Stock up on nonperishable ingredients for Christmas meals.

☆ Stock up on snacks and extra eggnog for surprise guests.

December 22–31

☆   Finish wrapping all presents.

☆   Clear space in the refrigerator.

☆   Tidy up the house and make room in closets for any house guests.

☆   Pick up turkey, ham, or other fresh meat for Christmas dinner.

☆   Relax by going to a movie or the *Nutcracker*, or take a drive to look at home decorations and lights.

☆   For Christmas Eve, see p. 177.

☆   For Christmas day, see p. 179.

CHAPTER III
The Just-for-Two Christmas

Whether you are newly married or just newly involved, holidays are tricky waters to negotiate. First of all, most likely you want to create a truly memorable celebration together. But the emotional pulls of the ways you each celebrated before you met are strong. Also, if you do come up with a plan that pleases you both, you may have to disappoint others in your families, and the guilt from breaking or bending established family traditions can be daunting.

GETTING STARTED

Talk to each other casually about the holidays, long before the pressure of plans are upon you. Sometime in October is ideal. Get to know what experiences your partner has had—good and bad. Listen to how the other is attached to Christmas but agree to make no definite plans or choices. Instead, let a plan emerge in this way:

Once you've chosen to celebrate Christmas together, each of you write down your memories (p. 6). Afterward, let each other know what memories come up during the exercise while one of you writes them down. Here is a sample list:

- Listening to Nat King Cole's Christmas album while trimming the tree
- Waking up before everyone else and opening the stocking that Santa had left by my bed
- Playing Handel's Messiah every Christmas Eve
- Listening to a recording of Dylan Thomas reading "A Child's Christmas In Wales" every Christmas Eve. We turned out the lights except those on the tree and listened
- Watching the lights being turned on in the tree in the park and having the neighbors over for desserts and cookies
- Watching the parade on TV
- Baking cookies—how it made the house smell sweet and feel warm
- The snowman contest on Christmas day and ice-skating the day after

Do this until the memories and reflections stop, perhaps thirty minutes or so. Then take a break before continuing—I suggest several hours or even a whole day. The pause gives you time to assimilate what you have heard and felt.

Now you are ready to talk about plans. Keep yourself receptive to different scenarios while you take turns sharing ideas and suggestions. One of you should write everything down. Your memories may have stirred longings to see your dad, to build snowmen, to have friends over for a screening of *It's a Wonderful Life*, to bake cranberry bread, to go caroling with the church chorale, to have a special gift exchange after midnight mass on Christmas Eve, or to fly off to the Caribbean and relax. Let the list of possibilities flow from your memories, without making any judgments or choices. Your ideas may be directly or only vaguely linked to memories. Don't worry. Don't judge. Take at least fifteen minutes to a half hour. If this is a true brainstorming session, your list will excite and delight you.

Then and only then talk about the responsibilities and obligations you both feel toward family and friends and try to formulate a plan that focuses on your own memories and longings while leaving room for obligations. For example, perhaps you choose to stay in with your partner on Christmas Eve instead of visiting your father. You can be with Dad on the day or night he trims his tree. When you trim your own tree, play your favorite Nat King Cole tape. Maybe friends and family you usually see at large family gatherings would like to go caroling with you *and* come to your house for desserts.

Don't be afraid to do something new that is all your own. Your new traditions will enrich rather than detract from established family traditions. The secret, however, is to think things through and communicate.

When I was working on this book a year ago, a friend decided that she was going to vacation in the Caribbean for two weeks at Christmas with her significant other. She realized that these plans were going to blow the current status quo relationship with her mother off the block. Since it was October, I encouraged her to disrupt the status quo. Don't be afraid. Communicate first, then trust the natural flow of events. There may be lots of pyrotechnics if one of your parents says, "How could you do this, isn't your family important?" Nevertheless, most relatives who are attached to set ways of celebrating Christmas will accept changes eventually.

You don't have to break tradition with an ax, however. If you are going away for Christmas, offer an alternative plan for an early celebration with family and friends. You could invite everyone over for presents and eggnog before you leave town. Have everyone bring a gift that doesn't cost more than $25 and do a grab bag. The point is, make sure you make time for your family and for yourselves.

Checklist for a Just-for-Two Christmas

The following checklist is a guide to help you move forward with your own plans once you've agreed on them. Use any part of it that you find helpful. Some couples keep a list like this in a handy spot and initial each item when it's completed.

❧ ─────────────────────────────

November 1–7

☆ Decide where and how you'll spend Thanksgiving, Christmas, and New Year's. If you are changing a major pattern in the family and/or extended family, such as going away or staying home together, changing the length of your stay with family or the time of your visit, tell all concerned *now*. Family members will adjust to a change in pattern better if you give them plenty of time. This is the week to break the news.

☆ Decide on what in-home entertaining, if any, you would like to do.

☆   Make a general list of all the physical tasks you need to accomplish over the next eight weeks.

☆   Agree to a general spending plan for the holidays, taking into consideration house/apartment decor, gifts, entertaining, special activities, and travel.

☆   Make your gift lists for each other (see p. 89) and the other people in your lives (see p. 74). Include home-made gifts such as cookies and jams (p. 103) and hand-made crafts (p. 119).

☆   For fresh flower gifts, now is the time to start the bulbs—amaryllis and paperwhites. For dried flowers and herbs, now is the time to select hydrangeas for drying. Now is also the time to collect pinecones, branches, and dried flowers for decorations.

☆   Collect baskets and tins for wrapping gifts from the kitchen.

☆   Shop for and begin to make craft gifts such as orna-ments, wreaths, and cards. (See p. 119.)

November 8–14
☆   Hang a special November/December calendar where you both can see it. Fill in the set events: concerts, office parties, vacation time/days off, parties at home or out, when or if to expect relatives, travel dates. Add your

own dates for gift and decoration shopping, buying and decorating the tree.

☆ Plan your entertaining menus and guest lists. (See p. 147.) Mail the invitations or invite people by phone.

☆ Order your turkey for Thanksgiving.

☆ Make any special reservations for car services, caterers, or house and pet sitters.

☆ Stock up on tape, film, batteries, stamps, ribbon, and wrapping paper.

☆ Shop for gifts on your list. (See "Shopping Tips," p. 92.)

☆ Buy or make Christmas cards.

November 15–21
☆ Start writing and addressing Christmas cards.

☆ Shop for gifts on your list.

☆ If you will be entertaining, see that you have enough china, serving bowls, and linens. Assemble holiday decorations and make a list of what you still need. Be sure to have plenty of candles on hand for the entire season.

☆ Stock up on frozen dinners or make some soups and chili to freeze for busy days ahead.

☆ Continue craft projects.

☆ Clean the house for Thanksgiving.

November 22–30
☆ Order gifts from catalogs. (See p. 95.)

☆ Shop for groceries for Thanksgiving.

☆ Decorate your house with a few autumnal branches, dried flowers, corn swags, or simple bowls of apples and pears.

☆ Prepare Thanksgiving feast and make extra cranberry sauce for gift giving. (See p. 113.)

☆ Set aside a corner, room, drawer, or closet for wrappings, gifts, and decor.

☆ Complete your gift shopping.

☆ Start baking Christmas cookies and freeze them until you're ready to package them for gifts.

December 1–7

☆ Make an Advent wreath (see p. 140) and place it in a central location.

☆ For the best selection, buy your tree now. (See p. 126.) Store it in a bucket of water in a cool place, such as the garage. Apartment dwellers should wait to buy their tree.

☆ Hang a wreath or swag on the door.

☆ Hang outdoor lights and/or window trim lights.

☆ Plan your holiday menus and assign potluck dishes, if any, to guests. (See p. 147.)

☆ Stock up on nonperishable supplies: wine, paper plates, and napkins.

☆ Complete Christmas baking and freeze.

☆ Complete any craft projects, including handmade stockings and ornaments.

December 8–14

☆ Decorate the inside of your house with garlands, Christmas cards, and candles.

☆   Wrap gifts for friends and family. (See p. 99.) Mail any that go out of town. Do this even if you will be with family—it saves you having to carry them as luggage.

☆   If you haven't already, buy your tree. (See p. 126.) Place it in a bucket of water until ready to trim.

☆   Check Christmas wardrobe and take to the cleaner's if necessary.

December 15–21

☆   Order special desserts or meats for Christmas dinner.

☆   Organize Christmas music for your CD or tape player. (See p. 171.)

☆   Trim the tree.

☆   Package and deliver gifts to neighbors, friends, and coworkers.

☆   Stock up on nonperishable ingredients for Christmas meals.

☆   Stock up on snacks and extra eggnog for surprise guests.

December 22–31

☆   Finish wrapping all presents.

☆   Clear space in the refrigerator.

☆   Tidy up the house and make room in closets for any house guests. If you are going to visit relatives, pack your luggage.

☆   Pick up turkey, ham, or other fresh meat for Christmas dinner.

☆   Relax by going to a movie, a concert, or a play.

☆   For Christmas Eve, see p. 177.

☆   For Christmas day, see p. 179.

CHAPTER IV
The Home-Alone Christmas

Christmas at home alone can be dreaded or welcomed. Either you don't want to be alone and are uneasy about having Christmas by yourself or you absolutely look forward to the whole experience. The factor common to both is that without family and familiar routines, holiday activities can be very difficult to think about, let alone plan and pull off. On the other hand, celebrating Christmas alone can be the most self-affirming time of your life, a profound gift of personal growth. For many people, the first Christmas alone is an opportunity to find out what the holiday really means and what makes it worth celebrating.

Planning for a Christmas alone requires as much thought as would planning with a large family. You need to be organized. Otherwise, you'll be buffeted by the demands, pressures, and pleasures of the season, all of which are truly inescapable. Christmas commercials bombard you on radio and TV; giant ads take over the daily papers; catalogs cram your mailbox; shop windows are elaborately decorated; friends and neighbors are full of Christmas conversation and invitations; office parties abound; and people on the street look expectant, excited, and even desperate.

Ignoring or "sliding" through Christmas actually might take more energy than creating a Christmas plan for yourself. Look at how much effort Ebenezer Scrooge put into ignoring the holiday. I've never counted the number of "Bah Humbugs" he barks and grumbles in the Dickens classic *A Christmas Carol*, but it is a relief when they are replaced with giddy merriness.

THE HOME-ALONE PLAN

Sometimes a person simply wants to go along with the pull of the season to be still and quiet at Christmastime. I have done it myself. But retreating from the public and exuberant world of Christmas must be as well thought out as plunging into it.

If you want time alone for Christmas, you must give it to yourself—set it aside, plan how and where you will use it, value and protect it, and, most important, communicate about it. Remember, during the Christmas season we all try to be altruistic and supportive of each other. Those close to you, who are probably imagining that you will be part of their Christmas, deserve to know that you're taking off to a cabin in the mountains for a private retreat, or to Nepal, or the Galapagos Islands, or that you'll simply be unplugging the phone for a few days.

It's a good idea to connect with loved ones before you retreat: cook for friends; hand-deliver gifts for parents and close relatives; devote some time to special people in your life. Then go ahead and luxuriate in your time alone. You will find that, if planned with consideration for yourself and others, a Christmas spent by yourself welcoming winter can be a very rewarding private experience.

Sometimes Christmas alone comes as a result of particular circumstances: A move to a distant city might make it logistically impossible to be with your loved ones. If this is the case, take time to sit quietly and think about how best to celebrate the Christmas passage.

I spent one of my first Christmases away from my California hometown in New York City, where I was struggling to get my writing/directing career going. I had neither the time nor the money to fly home. Apart from a little homesickness, I wasn't particularly sad about it all, but I didn't quite know how to celebrate on my own, either. I was poor and basically alone. Whatever I did, I knew it couldn't be extravagant.

I sat down one day in late November to write down my memories as described on p. 6, and discovered three cherished memories of my past Christmases:

1. Shared adventures with my family: taking a cabin in the mountains; going tobogganing and skiing; taking road trips to surprise unsuspecting relatives.
2. Church! I sang in the choir as a kid and loved the liturgical preparations and all the Christmas processions and rituals.
3. The Christmas I learned "it's more blessed to give." My dad came home a few nights before Christmas and told us that he had met a man who had no job, little money, and seven children. My dad asked us kids to go through our toys and games and give him what we didn't want and/or could part with. We wrapped our

offerings that night and my dad delivered the gifts anonymously.

After a few minutes, I had three good leads. First, I thought about how I might be able to have an adventure with my family and make it a Christmas present. I decided to take them around New York City with me during the holidays via tape recorder. None of them had ever been to New York, and I benefited from having a reason to get out and explore the city.

We went to Times Square to see the lights and to Rockefeller Center to watch the skaters and see the huge tree. The day I went there, a hundred tuba players were on the ice playing "Hark the Herald Angels Sing"!

I talked into the tape recorder constantly, trying to describe everything as it unfolded. I discovered that New Yorkers generally exhibit one of two responses to behavior extraordinaire, such as a young woman (me) talking into a black box. They either ignored me, probably suspecting that I was a bit "off," or they couldn't resist getting into the act. There were two men in Times Square, for example, who insisted upon saying hello and Merry Christmas to everybody in California.

We continued exploring—going everywhere—Central Park, Tavern on the Green, the Metropolitan Museum of Art. I described the bare trees surrounding the museum, the colorful banners high over the sun-drenched steps, the hot dog vendor and the steam coming from his cart, his gloves with no fingertips, and his hat that made him look like a Victorian street character.

Once inside the museum, I took us to the huge tree

and carved crêche in the medieval room where beautiful carols played softly and people spoke in hushed voices. I whispered descriptions of everything—the large and elegant angel ornaments; the figurines around the bottom of the tree that depicted an entire village of people surrounding the stable where Jesus was born, the excited faces of the shepherds running with small lambs slung over their shoulders toward a bright light shining upon the stable and manger, upon Mary and Joseph standing content amid the commotion.

In between my recorded adventures (I didn't try to do it in one day), I found a small church in Greenwich Village—St. Joseph's on 6th Avenue—where I felt instantly at home. I chose to attend services each Sunday of Advent, and volunteered for the Meals on Wheels home delivery for the next four Sundays.

My memories were beginning to resonate and create for me new shapes of Christmas in New York City. Close to Christmas, I made chili and cornbread and shared it with my next-door neighbors, Mike and Michael, who had been very helpful getting me settled. We trimmed the tree, which didn't take long since it was about eighteen inches high. I invited my neighbor on the other side over on Christmas night for the smallest roast turkey I'd ever seen. We ate and laughed and planned our futures.

If you are alone at Christmas, you have the unique opportunity to shape any kind of holiday you want. You can reach out and create an extended "family" by volunteering in a soup kitchen, in the YMCA Christmas tree lot, or by joining in on a neighborhood caroling walk or community sing-along.

Every year at Greenwich Village's St. Luke's in the Fields landmark church, the West Village Chorale sponsors just such a caroling walk. Sometimes two hundred people show up from all over the city: whole families, single people, groups, and individuals. Even pets are welcomed. People split into several groups to walk through the village, caroling restaurants, homes, shops, and bakeries. About an hour later everyone gathers back at the church for much more full-hearted singing and hot drinks and cookies.

Planning Tips for a Home-Alone Christmas

- Plan to do the things from your own experience that you particularly remember and love about Christmas. These are your anchors as well as your entryways into the season:

  Make an Advent wreath.

  Hang Christmas cards on the door.

  Make fudge and cookies on the Saturday before Christmas.

  Take a ride in the country.

  Go ice-skating on Christmas Eve.

  Pick one or two, and don't do anything you do not fondly remember. One woman I know, no matter where she is, goes to a Messiah Sing-along to get herself into the Christmas spirit.

- Do something for somebody else—for example, check in on an older neighbor and offer to run an errand. Reach out to somebody else who is alone and offer to cook. Do some Handmade Christmas

suggestions (p. 119); volunteer to serve Christmas
dinner at a soup kitchen or shelter.

- Plan ahead for the downtime that may occur. There
are books you want to read or projects to accomplish.
- Keep holiday entertaining simple—for example,
have friends in for soup and cider and tree trimming. Exchange small presents.
- Make a tape-recorded or videotaped Christmas
greeting for your loved ones who can't be with you
for Christmas. Keep track of time on the audio or
videotape—don't let it run too long.
- Plan to take an adventure: Ice-skate in the park; go
horseback riding; take a winter hike.
- Check local papers for listings of neighborhood
concerts and events and join in.

Checklist for a Home-Alone Christmas

November 1–7

☆ Write down your memories. (See p. 6.) List the ele-
ments of your perfect Christmas.

☆ Decide how you would like to spend Thanksgiving
and Christmas, and whom you would like to include.

☆ If you haven't already told them, and especially if
you know they are expecting you, tell your relatives and
friends that you'll be spending Christmas on your own
rather than joining them. You might want to share with

them the reason for this decision—money, job, responsibilities, travel, personal retreat.

☆ Make a general list of all the tasks you have to do before Christmas: shopping for gifts, groceries, and miscellaneous items; entertaining; mailing packages; baking; cleaning; decorating; buying the tree; making travel arrangements.

☆ If you will be traveling, make all hotel and car rental arrangements, and any other arrangements—confirm plane and train reservations. (See p. 46.)

☆ Decide on a spending plan for the holidays. Include gifts, decorations, entertaining, and travel.

☆ Make your gift list. (See p. 74.) Include any gifts you want to make: cookies, jams, and crafts such as wreaths and ornaments.

☆ Call local churches and hospitals or other charity organizations to find out about upcoming craft fairs, cookie fairs, caroling walks, open concerts, Christmas tree lots. Think about participating or, better yet, volunteering your services. Better still, get a couple of friends to volunteer with you.

☆ Now is also the time to collect pinecones, acorns, and branches for decorations.

☆ Collect baskets and containers for gifts from the kitchen. (See p. 103.)

☆ Shop for materials and begin to make craft gifts such as wreaths and ornaments and cards. (See p. 121.)

November 8–14
☆ Plan a supper and tree-trimming party for neighbors and friends. (See p. 147.) Make a guest list and menu ideas. Invite people by phone.

☆ Hang a special November/December calendar and fill in set events: concert dates, office parties, the start of vacation, deadlines for gift shopping and mailing, and any other social commitments or travel dates.

☆ Buy or make Christmas cards. (See p. 121.)

☆ If you are planning a party that requires caterers, book them now.

☆ Shop for gifts.

November 15–21
☆ Write and address Christmas cards.

☆ Look around your house or apartment and imagine a

few decorations—autumn branches for Thanksgiving; candles, wreaths, garlands, and the tree for Christmas. Get any decorations out of storage and check them over. Make a list of what else you need for decorations or entertaining.

☆   Buy needed tree decorations.

☆   Stock up on stamps, wrapping paper, tape, mailing boxes and envelopes, and gift tags.

☆   If you are hosting Thanksgiving dinner, shop for all nonperishables. If it's a potluck, let guests know what to bring.

☆   Complete craft projects.

November 22–30

☆   Call a nearby church or scout troop and volunteer a few hours in the Christmas tree lot.

☆   Order gifts from catalogs. (See p. 95.)

☆   Decorate your home with autumnal branches, sprigs, corn swags, dried flowers, branches, autumn mums, or a bowl of green apples.

☆   Buy the fresh goods for your Thanksgiving meal.

☆ Set aside a special Christmas corner for wrapping paper, gifts, and decorations.

☆ Complete your gift shopping. Start baking Christmas gifts. (See p. 103.)

☆ Buy any needed tree lights and/or ornaments. (See pp. 127–128.)

December 1–7

☆ Mail nonperishable gifts. Mail perishable gifts by December 15. Keep your gifts simple and warm. Don't try to make up for your absence with expensive gifts or complicated gadgets. Send warmth—gloves, caps, flannel shirts, p.j.'s, bath powder, cookies, and cakes.

☆ Mail Christmas cards.

☆ For best selection, buy your tree now. Store it in a cool place in a bucket of water. (See pp. 126–127.) Apartment dwellers will have to wait.

☆ Make an Advent wreath and place it somewhere central. (See p. 140.)

☆ Hang a wreath or swag on the door. (See p. 139.)

☆ Hang outdoor lights or window trim lights.

☆ Plan your Christmas dinner menus and/or assign potluck dishes to guests.

☆ Stock up on nonperishable supplies—wine, paper plates, and napkins.

☆ Complete baking gifts and freeze.

☆ Complete craft projects.

December 8–14

☆ Wrap gifts for friends and mail.

☆ Decorate indoors: garlands, Christmas cards, candles.

☆ If you haven't done so already, buy your Christmas tree.

☆ Decorate cookie ornaments.

☆ Order any special food for Christmas dinner.

December 15–21

☆　Buy fresh greens for swags, door wreaths, and bouquets.

☆　Have a tree-trimming party for friends.

☆　Deliver gifts to neighbors, friends, coworkers, and teachers.

☆　Stock up on nonperishable ingredients for Christmas meals.

☆　Stock up on extra goodies—snacks for unexpected guests.

☆　Buy or pick up turkey or ham.

December 22–31

☆　Complete all gift-wrapping.

☆　Check Christmas wardrobe.

☆　Do a final clean-up of house or apartment.

☆　Firm up plans for after Christmas.

☆   Relax by going to a movie, or taking a drive in the country or a walk through the neighborhood.

☆   For Christmas Eve, see p. 177.

☆   For Christmas day and Christmas night, see pp. 179–180.

☆   Call home.

CHAPTER V
The Traveler's Christmas

According to statistics, few large families (two adults and two or more children) actually travel for pleasure at Christmas— that is, travel purely for the purpose of exploring or being in a place other than home for the holidays. If large families *do* travel, it's to familiar places where relatives live— quite often to those who live in popular *warm* locales.

One reason that so few families travel for pleasure at Christmas is pretty obvious—it's expensive; more expensive than at any other time of the year. Even if hotels or motels offer discounted rates, which by and large they do not, they are discounting from an already inflated holiday rate. And plane fares, if not booked long in advance at special rates, can soak up an entire family holiday budget and then some.

Single adults and couples without children, and non-traditional families, such as one adult with one or two children, are more likely to travel for pleasure at Christmas. The timing is perfect since most schools are closed for one or two weeks and adults can arrange vacations from work far in advance.

Domestic destinations include mountain and skiing resorts, warm-weather and tourist-friendly cities such as Los Angeles, San Diego, San Francisco, and Orlando, where there are many family-friendly hotels. Disney World has recently opened the All Star Hotel, which puts up any size family for about $70 a night.

Native American sites in the Southwest such as Albuquerque, Taos, and Santa Fe, New Mexico, are also popular at Christmastime.

Modes of transportation include everything from camper to jet. Adults and children alike are fascinated by trains, especially for short jaunts through snowy winter terrain. Train travel is relatively inexpensive as well as pleasurable during the holidays, and Amtrak offers special promotions where kids travel for a reduced fare.

International trips include popular European rail excursions through Switzerland and Scandinavia, and Viarail, Canada's incredible rail journey through some of the most beautifully rugged territory of North America.

The Yucatán Peninsula of Mexico and Jamaica and other islands in the Caribbean are popular not only because of warm weather but because the native population is predominantly Catholic and the holidays are jam-packed with traditional festivals and religious pageantry. In Jamaica, the Boxing Day parade, held on the first weekday after Christmas, is as lively as carnival in the spring. In Mexico, Las Posada processions outdoors each day start on December 12 and continue through Christmas day.

Another popular international Christmastide destination is southern Germany, for quaint Bavarian towns, handmade gifts from charmingly decorated shops, sweets and hearty foods, festivals, concerts, and pageants. In London, there's the promise of a Dickensian Christmas, replete with wafting aromas of roast beef and plum pudding. Greece offers the possibility of two Christmases, one week apart: one Catholic, the other Greek Orthodox.

In Montreal and especially Quebec, tourists may hear French carols in Gothic cathedrals and enjoy nearby ski-ing, too.

❧❧ ❧❧ ❧❧

PLANNING THE TRIP

If you think that a travel Christmas is exactly what you and yours would like, start making plans early—a year in advance will help secure good rates to the more popular destinations. But before you rush off to a travel agent or start calling tourist boards, consider just what it is that you want: What is your primary purpose? What part of your curiosity or appetite are you seeking to express by taking a journey at Christmastime?

- Do you want an adventure and a chance to spend quality time with your child or your loved one? If so, you might want to hike the Indian ruins of the Southwest, ski a Colorado or Idaho mountain, or take off for the Galapagos.
- Do you want peaceful relaxation in the warmth somewhere? Consider Hawaii, the Caribbean, the Yucatán, or any of the Club Meds that offer warm-weather R&R.
- Do you want to experience Christmas in another culture? Perhaps a train trip through parts of Europe (Eurail adventures in Europe) to hear the choirs of Vienna or Mozart performed in Prague on Christ-mas Eve; to shop in Paris and attend services at

Nôtre Dame; to indulge in a traditional smorgasbord in Scandinavia; to watch the fine glass blowers, carvers, and craftpersons in the small towns of southern Germany.

You might dance through the upbeat festivals of the Caribbean, dine in a Victorian setting in England or Wales, hike to the great waterfalls of South America, march in a Las Posada procession in Mexico, or be among all the other pilgrims in Bethlehem on Christmas Day.

Sit down and write down your fantasy Christmas destinations and dream travel activities. Do not censor your list at all, or make it make sense yet. You do not need to justify your travel yens and cravings. Put the list aside for a while.

Consider your finances and prepare a spending/savings plan with your significant others that will allow you to afford a Christmas travel vacation.

Choose one or two dream trip ideas from your fantasy list. Try to combine your fantasy with the fantasies of your significant others until you hone your dream to one or two ideas. If you are traveling with children, remember that international travel with children can be a nightmare unless there are activities that will interest them during travel and after arrival. The destination has to be good for children or the precious time set aside to "be together" will be fruitless.

Now, find yourself a travel agent who is a certified specialist in your areas of interests: For example, my agent, Dean Klopsis, at Odyssey Travel is not only a certified family travel specialist, he's also a nature/adventure travel specialist with great expertise in handling special or exotic holiday needs.

There are as many travel specialists as there are tastes and curiosities: food travel specialists for those interested in international cooking schools, restaurants, famous vineyards, and marketplaces; family pleasure–travel specialists for those interested in family-friendly travel; art travel specialists for those interested in the great museums, birthplaces, and memorials to famous artists. The list of travel agent specialties goes on to include history, music, theater, architecture, textiles and crafts, ecotourism, and gardens. You can even find an agent who specializes in romantic travel.

Other agents are expert at handling the special needs of single adults with kids, large families, mature travelers, disabled travelers, young newlyweds, single adults, and gay and lesbian travelers.

To find such an agent, look up your local chapter of the American Society of Travel Agents (ASTA), which certifies agents for specialty travel. There are over 127,000 members around the world, and ASTA, which is about sixty-five years old, has chapters in several major cities. The ASTA headquarters is in Arlington, Virginia; phone (703) 739-2782.

Before you call an agent, do your homework and have specifics ready to present. For example:

- You are parents of two teenagers and you want a Christmas tour of the Southwest, or London, or Munich, or Paris.
- You are a single person with a ten-year-old who

loves animals; you both want to go somewhere near the water so that you can swim; and you want to be warm.

- You are a musician, and you and your significant other want to hear Christmas music in the great cathedrals of the world.
- You are a bungee-jumper, and you and your adult son want to jump the cliffs of South America for Christmas.
- You are newly married, and the two of you want to go someplace to be alone; it doesn't matter where, but it has to be romantic, beautiful, and serene with a warm tradition of Christmas *and* a night life.

It may take a few go rounds with your travel agent—browsing brochures, making compromises if necessary—but once your travel plans are in place, you are free to plan Christmas on the home front. And Christmas at home is important—it is the opportunity to exchange warmth and express affection for all the friends, relatives, coworkers, teachers, and neighbors who will not be traveling with you but with whom you want to share some holiday pleasure. Just make sure your Christmas-at-home festivities are completed no less than three days before you leave on your trip.

Checklist for a Traveler's Christmas

March 1–15

☆ Decide where and how you would like to travel during the Christmas holidays. For domestic or international travel bargains to one of the more popular destinations, such as Orlando, Los Angeles, San Francisco, Munich, Vienna or London, book your flight, hotel, and car rental now for low fares. Choose to depart on off-peak days and hours to avoid heavy crowds and higher fares. Although most national and international destinations can be booked at the last minute, the earlier you book, the better the fares.

☆ Set up a travel savings/spending plan.

☆ Coordinate school vacations and work vacations times.

October 15–21

☆ If you haven't done so already, book flights for all domestic and international travel. It's still possible to get the flight you need but probably not at discounted fares.

☆ Decide how you will spend the holidays before you leave home and what in-home entertaining you will do. Include Thanksgiving in this discussion—how big an affair do you want for each event?

☆ If you haven't done so already, communicate to all extended family and friends your plans to be away at Christmas.

☆ Arrange for house, pet, and plant sitters while you will be away.

❧ ━━━━━━━━━━━━━━━━━━━━━━━━━━━━━

October 22–28
☆ Confirm hotel/motel/car rental reservations that you made last spring, or book reservations now. Ask for confirmation numbers and/or faxed copies of confirmations.

☆ Make a general list of all the tasks you must accomplish over the next few weeks. This might include simple home decorations, outdoor lights, tree, Christmas cards, gift shopping, preparations for in-home entertaining, making gifts such as cookies and crafts; grocery shopping; buying anything you might need while you're traveling; mailing packages; house cleaning; attending school plays, office parties, or concerts; packing.

☆ Set a spending plan for the holidays, taking into consideration house decor, gifts, entertaining, special activities plus your travel spending plan.

☆ Make your gift lists. (See p. 74.) Include homemade gifts such as cookies, breads, and preserves. (See p. 103.)

❧

October 29–November 4

☆ Hang a special November/December/January calendar that's easy to see. Fill in events and deadlines such as school plays, concerts, parties, house decorating day; gift shopping (start and complete); activities with the kids; shopping for the trip; trip arrangements and packing; vacation dates, plane, train, or car departures and arrivals.

☆ Plan your pre-Christmas party menu/and guest list. Mail invitations or invite people by phone.

☆ Make any reservations for baby-sitters, car services, or caterers, if needed.

☆ Stock up on tape, film, batteries, stamps, ribbon, and wrapping paper.

☆ Start making handmade ornaments to give as gifts or keep for your own. (See p. 119.)

❧

November 5–11

☆ Shop for gifts.

☆ Take out boxes of holiday decorations and special tableware from storage. Replace faded or broken items, and buy fresh candles. Check Christmas lights.

☆ Cook and freeze some make-ahead meals for busy times coming up—two or three hearty soups, chilis, or casseroles.

☆ Plan Thanksgiving menu. If you are having a potluck, let guests know what to bring.

☆ Confirm plans, if any, with caterers for Christmas party.

☆ Buy or make Christmas cards.

November 12–18

☆ Order turkey or pies for Thanksgiving.

☆ If you haven't done so already, order gifts from catalogs to be sent directly to recipients.

☆ Decorate your house with autumnal branches, dried corn swags, or bouquets of dried flowers.

☆ Complete your gift shopping.

☆ Take in any clothes that need to be dry cleaned for trip. Buy any items needed for the trip.

☆ Watch videos or read travel information about Christmas at your planned destination.

November 19–30

☆ Arrange to have your mail and newspaper stopped while you will be away.

☆ Buy the fresh groceries for Thanksgiving dinner. Make extra cranberry sauce for gifts. (See p. 113.)

☆ Buy wrapping paper, tape, tags, scissors, mailing boxes, and envelopes. Buy any needed home decor items and Christmas lights.

☆ Set aside a corner, room, drawer, or closet for wrappings, gifts, and decor.

☆ Plan your pre-Christmas party menu and assign potluck dishes, if any, to guests.

☆ Wrap gifts.

December 1–7

☆ Buy a small tree or large wreath and set it up indoors. (See p. 125.)

☆ Hang a wreath or swag on the door. (See p. 138.)

☆ Hang outdoor lights, hooked to an automatic timer.

☆   Stock up on nonperishable supplies such as wine, canned foods, and paper goods for your Christmas party.

☆   Enjoy one handmade project: gingerbread ornaments, cookies, handmade ornaments, gifts from the kitchen. (See p. 103, 119.)

☆   Stock up on snacks for "drop-in" guests.

December 8–14
☆   Hang or place some decorations indoors: garlands, Christmas cards, candles . . .

☆   Trim the tree.

☆   Mail any packages to be shipped. If you are traveling to visit relatives, send presents ahead, as well.

☆   Do last-minute gift or trip shopping.

☆   If you haven't done so already, take out suitcases (one per person) and pack main items for trip. Do not pack medicine, jewelry, business papers, passports, or cash in your luggage to be checked.

❦

December 15–21

☆   Deliver gifts to neighbors and friends, teachers, and coworkers.

☆   Go over details with house-sitters. Make sure they know to take in any mail or handouts that might accumulate, and to water plants, including the Christmas tree.*

❦

Day of Travel

☆   Call the airlines to confirm your flight time before you leave for the airport.

☆   Arrive at airport at least one hour before domestic departures, two hours for international flights. If you are carrying gifts, know that they are subject to security inspection, which could involve unwrapping them. To avoid the delay and aggravation, pack gifts in checked luggage.

---

* It's my own personal preference to come home to the tree and some remnant of Christmas. You may want to take everything down before you go. However, outdoor lights and indoor lights on a timer are good deterrents to would-be burglars.

CHAPTER VI
The Last-Minute Christmas

It's December 18 and you haven't done a thing to prepare for Christmas—you've no plan; no wreath, no cards, no tree, and certainly no gifts. You've enjoyed the Christmas cards and gifts that you've been receiving, all the while feeling increasingly guilty because you haven't sent any out. But what can you do? You might be depressed about something—your job, your family relationships, something. And you don't have enough time, money, or enthusiasm to get into Christmas this year.

This happens to the best of us—especially if we've had a difficult change in life. It also can happen to anybody working under the pressure of a deadline, which leaves no time to think, buy, decorate, or spend. What makes matters worse is that once you miss out on the holiday spirit, you can fall prey to an array of negative feelings that leave you constantly annoyed and cranky.

By December 18, you may feel as if you're a victim of Christmas. Those never-ending carols follow you everywhere—at the cleaner's, the supermarket, and the gas station. Even in the hardware store, where you usually can depend on grumpy service, choirs or crooners are incessantly singing "Angels We Have Heard on High." The sidewalks, parking lots, and stores are abuzz with that killer-bee energy of shoppers. And it begins to scare you.

Friends have invited you to gatherings, and though you've said you'd go, you're planning how to back out gracefully. You can't help yourself. You are a yuletide hostage; you can neither be in Christmas nor out of it.

Then something happens. Well, if you are lucky, it does. Having just such a December 18 following a difficult breakup several years ago, I was walking lock-jawed and glum down my block, when I saw an old man slip and nearly fall. His cane went flying and his grocery bag tumbled, spilling canned goods and what looked like an Entenmann's cake.

A young man walking his dog not only stopped to help but offered to see the old man home. The old man took the young man's arm, the black labrador walked attentively alongside.

I was touched by this scene: The scare of slipping and losing control and the humiliation of spilled groceries (as far as I'm concerned, one's grocery bag is as private as one's underwear drawer) were met with warm and assuring strength and patience.

As the two men and dog disappeared around the corner, I became keenly aware that I was standing still, probably for the first time in weeks. Then I noticed the quiet wind in the few bushy evergreens amid the line of bare gray maples. Down on the corner where men were selling Christmas trees and wreaths, I saw fire leaping from a large metal drum. There was always a fire going while the men worked outside hoisting trees into the baling machines before sending them home with customers. But in this moment, that particular fire, from half a block away, warmed me through. I could make out the tinny strains of "The First Noel" coming from their battered tape player, and the spirit hit me like an electrical surge. Here is how my own Last-Minute Christmas unfolded.

Like Ebenezer awakening on Christmas morning, I became uncontrollably enthused. I wanted to buy a wreath and a tree on the spot, to run to the butcher and buy the goose in the window, to rampage the toy store and buy harmonicas and trumpets, Etch-a-Sketches, Slinkys, board games, Patty Playpals and G.I. Joes. Instead, I bought an armload of evergreen branches and sprinted home. With the aromatic pine boughs in a pitcher of water in front of me, I sat down to organize my newfound enthusiasm into a plan for Christmas.

MEMORY

No matter when you begin to plan for Christmas, always begin by writing down your memories. Sit quietly and let your thoughts flow. It is essential that you do this, especially if you are facing a last-minute Christmas. Whatever shape Christmas takes, it should come from within as a personal expression and not from the barrage of stimuli and demands in the outer world.

As soon as I had my memory list to look over, I began to make a "possibles list," all those things I actually could pull off that would connect me with my memories: a tree, wreath, and ornaments; having friends over to help trim the tree, string cranberries, have mulled cider, snacks, and Christmas cookies, and watch a video—perhaps *It's a Wonderful Life;* send plates of cookies as gifts to friends;

midnight mass at the cathedral or the festival of carols at St. Tim's; Christmas day—quiet; Christmas night, dinner with friends; fly home on the 27th for a surprise visit and those long talks with family that I cherish.

Next, I brainstormed a possible gift list. Then I set everything aside while I looked at my financial resources and came up with a spending plan for all of Christmas—entertaining, gifts, and all.

THE PLAN

Finally, and not too long after I had sat down to do it, a satisfying but manageable plan for a last-minute Christmas emerged. It was a Christmas I could enjoy, familiar but also with room for new traditions and surprises. And my plan wouldn't exhaust my budget: A sketch of it follows:

- A small tree-trimming party involving dinner, stringing cranberries and popcorn for the tree, and watching *Miracle on 34th Street*, *A Christmas Memory*, or *It's a Wonderful Life*.
- An under-$10 gift grab bag. Extra gifts in case anyone brings a child.
- Borrow a camcorder to tape the tree-trimming party. Send the videotape as a Christmas card to family.
- Christmas Eve at the cathedral for midnight mass.
- Christmas day, quiet. Christmas dinner with friends.

- Quick gifts—gift certificates, catalog deliveries (new p.j.'s), tins of bakery-bought cookies.
- Fly home on December 27 and back on Jan 1.

My plan came off pretty much as planned, except that the tree-trimming party was so enjoyable nobody wanted to sit and watch a video. Instead we sang along to some classic albums: Elvis, Nat King Cole, and Mitch Miller.

The gift grab bag ended up being a terrific idea. People brought great presents: puzzles, wind-up toys, wild socks and T-shirts, tiny joke books and quote books, nifty mugs and key chains with whistles. There was a Slinky, which everyone passed around, a kaleidoscope, and refrigerator magnets. Negotiating trades was allowed and everybody, especially the kids, made trades. One gift certificate for a twenty-minute neck and shoulder rub was lobbied heavily for trade.

The videotaped Christmas greeting for my relatives was a great idea. Several people at the party knew their way around video cameras so the camera person was always changing and the resulting forty-five-minute tape was fun to watch.

Midnight mass at the cathedral on Christmas Eve held lots of surprises. I talked two friends into going with me, and they were delighted. The mass began with a marching band and procession of the world-renowned Bread and Puppet Theatre's twenty-foot-high ceremonial puppets.

I felt very lighthearted on Christmas day, and kept to myself, just as I wanted. For lunch I had leftover soup from the tree-trimming party. I made a few phone calls to friends and relatives, then managed to make a chocolate cake, my contribution to Christmas dinner, and took a nap before going off to my friends' house.

Even though it was planned at the last minute, this celebration brought some of the excitement, joy, and peace of Christmas into my life. The experience proved to me that even if I wait until the last minute, somehow I manage to get into the spirit of things.

So, take heart! Even though things might not be going well for you, and you haven't labored in high spirits during the monthlong preparations, you can still give wing, at any moment, to the part of your soul that yearns to fly into Christmas.

Checklist for a Last-Minute Christmas

A checklist, which people use to thwart panic and confusion, is essential when you're planning a last-minute Christmas. The following checklist is a sample based on my own last-minute plans, but reviewing it may help you shape and focus your own list. Your own last-minute plans might involve more or fewer get-togethers, no religious ceremonies, a lot more shopping, whatever. The most important thing to remember is to keep plans simple and rooted in personal memory and taste.

December 18

☆   Take fifteen minutes to draw upon memories so that this last-minute Christmas still can be uniquely and fully yours, full of your personal character and touches. (See "Honoring Memories," p. 6.)

☆   Decide how you want to spend the remaining holidays, especially Christmas Eve, Christmas Day, and New Year's. Plan at least one special activity with friends and family or chosen loved ones.

☆   Make travel arrangements—plane/bus/train reservations, car rental, motel/hotel reservations.

☆   Make a list of tasks in order of priority and possibility: shopping for gifts, decorations, and a tree; having friends over for supper and tree-trimming; grocery shopping; house cleaning; gift wrapping; packing; getting a pet sitter if you are traveling.

☆   Make gift list.

☆   If you can afford to do so, use catalogs to order cakes, fruit, gift baskets, sweaters, pajamas, or any other item as gifts for family and friends. Have the gifts sent overnight or second-day delivery. (See "Shopping by Phone," p. 95.)

☆   Call friends to invite them over for supper, tree-trimming, screening of Christmas movies, and grab-bag gift exchange (under $10 and wrapped) on December 22.

☆   Accept an invitation you have left unanswered.

☆   Take any Christmas decorations out of storage and hang them up.

☆   Make arrangements for Christmas Eve: midnight mass, concert, ceremony of carols, dinner at a restaurant, travel.

December 19

☆   Buy tree and extra lights and ornaments if needed. (See pp. 125–129.) Buy popcorn and cranberries for stringing. Buy extra boughs of greens for fresh bouquets.

☆   Shop for gifts and wrapping paper, ribbon tape, tissue paper, tags, bags, tins and boxes, extension cords.

☆   Buy groceries, paper goods, and decorations for tree-trimming party.

☆   Order Christmas cookies from the bakery—enough to serve at the party and to send home as presents.

☆   Reserve videos for rental on December 22.

☆   Make arrangements for pet sitter for December 27 to January 1.

December 20

☆   String lights on the tree and place branches of greens decoratively around in pitchers.

☆   Decorate door with a swag of fresh greens and a red bow.

☆   Select Christmas music for tree-trimming party.

☆   Complete wrapping presents for UPS to pick up for out-of-town shipping.

December 21

☆   Do last-minute party shopping: candles, film, batteries, party favors, tablecloth.

☆   Pick up cookies from bakery. Put extras on plates or in tins to give as gifts.

☆   Buy fresh greens for party salad.

☆   Finish wrapping presents.

☆   Prepare soup for tree-trimming party; refrigerate.

☆   Clean house.

❧

December 22
☆   Call UPS to arrange pickup of video Christmas card on December 23.

☆   Set up buffet table. (See p. 169.)

☆   Pick up sourdough bread from bakery.

☆   Select Christmas music (see p. 171) and pick up videos.

☆   Organize ornaments for tree trim.

☆   Arrange food on buffet table.

☆   During the party, let everyone shoot a few minutes on the camcorder as a Christmas greeting for the family.

❧

December 23
☆   Send video Christmas card via UPS or FedEx. For about $25 your family can receive the "card" next day.

☆   Complete gift shopping and wrapping.

☆   Do any shopping for Christmas Eve or Christmas day meals.

❄️ ─────────────────────────────────────

December 24–25
☆ Watch *Miracle on 34th Street*.

☆ Attend the ceremony of carols and then midnight mass at the cathedral.

☆ Sleep in on Christmas day. Make cake for dinner dessert.

☆ Dinner at friends' house on Christmas night.

❄️ ─────────────────────────────────────

December 26–30
☆ Buy Christmas cards and send for New Year's greetings instead!

☆ Pack for trip home.

Part II

CHRISTMAS DETAILS AND CHECKLISTS

CHAPTER VII
Gifts and Giving

A gift is a symbol that says you hold a particular someone in your heart and you wish to assure them that they'll always have a place there.

Christmas presents are different from all other occasion gifts—birthday, anniversary, even surprise I-just-love-you gifts. They have a particular mission—to treat the senses, raise the spirits, delight and spin the hearts of both the recipient and the giver; and to carry a message of loyalty and gratitude.

It's no wonder we sometimes get a little nervous about giving the perfect gift.

COMING UP WITH THE PERFECT PERSONAL GIFT

In his long, delicious poem "A Child's Christmas in Wales," Dylan Thomas describes the "useful" and "useless" presents of Christmas morning. Those useful ones—engulfing mufflers, mittens, nose cozies, and books that "tell all about the wasp except why," are no match for the so-called useless "bag of jelly babies, folded flag, false nose, tram conductor's cap, celluloid duck, painting book . . . toffee, fudge, marzipan . . . troops of tin soldiers who if they could not fight could always run, rubber snakes, hobby games for little engineers . . . a whistle to make the dogs bark to wake the old man next door to make him rap on the wall, and a packet of pink-tipped sugar cigarettes."

Thomas remembers which presents delight him, even thirty years later. It's the so-called useless presents—whose sole purpose is to surprise and inspire—that complete the mission of the Christmas present. They bring joy to the moment and to the world of that twelve-year-old boy.

None of us wants to give or get gifts that only fill a mundane need. We want our gift to work a tiny bit of magic, to be the one someone would write a poem about. We want to give spontaneously from the heart and have our gift received exuberantly. But, to paraphrase the character Paul Buchman of the hit TV series *Mad About You,* "It's *not always* going to happen, my friend."

There are a few obstacles. First of all, in many family giving traditions, not all gifts can be surprises. Aunt Lucy counts on that expensive French bath powder your mother gives her every Christmas, and seems to make it last until December 24. And your brother-in-law, Bob, counts on the marmalade and sugared pecans you make only at Christmastime. I count on my friend David to renew my magazine subscription to *Harpers* that he started up for me five years ago. And he counts on his mother's GAP gift certificate for a fresh supply of T-shirts and jeans.

In every family, certain traditional exchanges must go on—fruit cakes, smoked meats and cheeses, Fruit of the Month subscriptions, decorated boxes of homemade but-

ter toffee, fudge, jars of marmalade, chutneys, gift certificates, wool gloves, flannel pajamas, special coffees, and
saltwater taffy. I would not advise trying to change pat-
terns just for the joy of giving something different. All of
these presents are treats, and even though they may not
surprise, and giving the same thing every year may get a
little boring, Uncle Allen still relishes and craves the
smoked ham. And as for Aunt Lucy, that bath powder is,
well . . . more than bath powder. If you were to change
it to a subscription to *Newsweek,* for example, you might
really spoil her Christmas.

Another obstacle between you and the perfect gift is
the perfection mind-set. Obsessing about getting the perfect gift can get in the way of your delight in giving,
which you need in order to choose a wonderful gift.

A few Christmases ago, my friend Nancy Creal, who
contributed much to this book, gave her nephew the perfect gift. She knew he was interested in magic and, feeling
acutely tuned into his wants and pleasures, she bought
and wrapped a magic kit for him.

But, alas, the magic kit was way below the boy's expertise and interest. When he laughed at it, saying "how
infantile," Nancy felt like throttling him.

But she realized that when you don't live with a child,
you end up choosing a gift for your idea of the child
rather than for the real child. Nancy had invested the
wrong part of herself in shopping for her nephew. Want-
ing so badly to get "the right gift" separated her from her
own delight and humor. She resolved not to work so hard
to intuit "the perfect or right gift" again.

The following year, when shopping for her nephew,

she took along the kid inside herself—that is, her readiness to be delighted and to follow that delight. At a natural history museum in Connecticut, she was impressed by an actual dinosaur footprint. For a nominal fee, visitors could take plaster molds of a footprint mold. Nancy made a copy of the big footprint and sent it to her nephew for Christmas. They still talk about it as the best present ever given, ever received.

Perhaps the last obstacle to a spontaneous and perfect gift is the fear that your gift will go unused. When this fear goes unchecked, it leads to Weed Wackers, garbage disposals, and snow shovels with red bows under the tree. These eminently useful presents should wait (unless specifically requested). Instead, stir the heart of the gardener with a beautiful book or CD/ROM on world gardens and gardening techniques along with several packets of flower seeds and a subscription to a gardening magazine. Or for TV fans who have requested something as useful as a subscription to *TV Guide*, add a surprise—tickets to a taping of their favorite TV show, or really wow them with multimedia software so they can make their own TV show.

FIVE STEPS TO GREAT SHOPPING

You should take five important steps before you leave the house, pick up the phone, or log onto any online computer service to buy a gift. And because many people run out to the mall before doing them, they collapse under the task. These steps, when spread out over a couple of days, give your creativity time to simmer and cook up delicious gift ideas. The five steps are:

1. List
2. Brainstorm
3. Plan spending
4. Imagine
5. Choose

List

No matter when you get around to the gift detail, do this step first. Put on some Christmas music. Have notebook and pencil ready. This first step gets ideas out of your head and onto paper. You will feel lighter and more focused the minute after you do this. In a large notebook, make a master list of all the people you want to give gifts to. Leave room next to their names for other information, such as any hints they've dropped, how much you can spend, and what you've decided on. But first, just list names and if they've actually said what they want for Christmas. A sample layout follows.

Master Christmas List

	WANTS	CAN SPEND	WHAT
Mom	everybody to be happy		
Dad			
John	tool box	$40	
Jim	VIDEO RENTAL GUIDE		
Sharon			
Barbara			
Annie			
Kate	WIND CHIMES		
Phillip & George			
Gordon & B.J.	A WEEKEND AWAY		
Helen & Hank			
Jon	BIRD FEEDER		

Brainstorm

Next, at the top of a separate page, write the person's name again, then brainstorm. For the next five or ten minutes, write as quickly as you can all the things you know about the person—job, birth sign, likes, dislikes, personality quirks, hobbies, character traits, tastes, your particular memories. Be sure to include what, if anything, the people have told you they want for Christmas.

That's all you do. Don't try to make sense; incomplete sentences and phrases are fine. Even if you think you know this person very well, put everything down on paper so you can look at it.

Spending Plan

After brainstorming on each person on your list, consult your finances and plan how much you'll spend on gifts. Remember, of course, to consider other financial demands, such as Christmas travel and entertaining. Next to each name on your master list, write the amount you can afford to spend on each person.

Imagine

Look at everything you've written about the person on your brainstorm page. Circle the things that trigger your imagination. In this way, the page will lead you to ideas for a gift. Write them down as they occur.

For example, a friend emerges from my brainstorm page as an enthusiastic do-it-yourself guy who enjoys restoring Volkswagen Beetles. He reads biographies. He loves hosting big family picnics, going out to the movies, having pizza on the run and riding his mountain bike. He's crazy about pro basketball, rock and roll concerts, sweet desserts, computers, and one-hour massages. He complains about not having enough unstructured time to spend with loved ones or with himself. He plays the lottery regularly.

Here are gift ideas that come to mind:

Warm/practical: a new tool box packed with small surprises, such as a book he's been dying to read, a framed photo of the most recent family picnic, a computer organizer/date book.

Budget fun: a candy-striped popcorn box packed with a supply of Milk Duds, M&Ms, Raisinettes, and a book of movie passes or gift certificates for the video store.

Extravagant fun: a certificate for one free pizza along with two tickets to a pro basketball game packed inside an empty (clean) pizza box.

Sweet: two dozen homemade cookies shaped like Volkswagen Beetles, packed in a colorful tin with a lottery ticket, or a subscription to the Chocolate of the Month club, attached.

Hip: a tee-shirt from the Apollo Theater in Harlem, New York City, where some of his favorite rock and roll and R&B groups debuted. Include a CD collection of hits from the '60s.

Special: a handmade certificate promising an ANY-THING-CAN-HAPPEN DAY of unstructured time in which I am available to be with him or baby-sit or cover for him while he spends time alone.

Comforting: a bottle of body oil with a gift certificate good for a one-hour massage at the gym or spa.

Sporty: new bicycle gloves and a book on bicycle trails in the beautiful areas nearby.

Friendly: a Bulls sweatshirt or warm gloves.

Choose

Once you've written your ideas down, circle the ones that are possible and eliminate those that are beyond your budget. If you don't like any of your ideas, go back to brainstorming. Most likely, something will emerge as a wonderful, personal gift that you can afford to buy. Make your choice.

Now you're ready to shop.

WISH LISTS FOR KIDS

If you haven't begun a gift book for the kids in your life, there's no time like now to start. An $8^{1}/_{2} \times 11$ inch notebook with a record of their wish lists and gifts from year to year not only helps you stay organized, it's a great gift to give them once they've grown up. Their history of wishes and presents can be as charming as height marks on the kitchen wall.

For very young children, usually it's best to put off gathering wishes until the first week of December, when the excitement of Christmas begins to build. When I was small, we wrote letters to Santa during the first week of December listing all our wishes. They were secret and sealed and my parents "mailed" them for us.

In Germany and other European countries, kids write a wish list, roll it up, and put it in their shoe, which they leave outside their bedroom door on the eve of the feast of St. Nicholas on December 6. In the morning, if the list is gone and there's a piece of candy in the shoe, the child has St. Nick's ear, at least. If the list is gone and there is a rock or twig in the shoe, St. Nick is leaving a warning. If the child doesn't correct some bad behavior, St. Nick isn't going to give his or her wish list another look.

The way wish lists are made can change as kids grow up. Santa letters and wish lists for St. Nick can become notes left where they'll be seen. One family I know has a decorated wish box, like a suggestion box, with little scraps of paper next to it. All the kids can put in as many wishes for themselves as they like, but they must put in three wishes for someone else. No peeking—ever.

There are all kinds of things you can do to make dropping hints fun: leave notes where people will find them, such as inside the coffee canister, toothbrush holder, medicine cabinet, pocket, on the computer screen, on the keyboard . . .

GIFT IDEAS FOR KIDS

If you live apart from the kids on your list and feel out of touch with them, remember you can count on the toys that pleased you years ago. Most are still popular today: Mr. Potato Head, Slinky, Etch-a-Sketch. Board games such as Sorry and Monopoly are still okay, too. Other no-fail gifts for kids include:

- Dinosaurs: toys, books, videos, or CD/ROM for age ten and under.
- Any kind of scope: microscopes, telescopes, kaleidoscopes. Kids love seeing the world up close and in a new way.
- Video and hand-held computer games: especially the newest.
- Books about anything the child is interested in—animals, airplanes, nature, science, Africa, computers . . .
- Disposable cameras with the developing prepaid. A great gift from grandparents or any adult living away from the child. Send it with instructions for taking pictures that show what the child cares about in the house, on the block, at school.
- Subscription to the Nickelodeon channel on TV.
- Puzzle maps and globes and anything to do with geography are good for ages nine to thirteen.
- Erector sets and Lego building kits.
- Sports equipment: basketballs, baseball gloves, hockey sticks, footballs, tennis rackets, inline skates, Ping Pong paddles and table, badminton sets, and sporting equipment. Also sports clothes such as sweats and team jerseys or sweatshirts for the enthusiastic sports kid.
- Personal electronics: radios and tape players.
- Radio control toys.
- Techno-gifts, such as computer software, or CD/ROM. Ask your kid's teacher or at a computer store.
- Brainstorms Catalog. (See p. 97.) I like this idea, because kids ten and older love looking through it.

Roll one up, tie it with a bow, and put it in their stockings. Give them a handmade gift certificate toward science toys, books, building sets, or T-shirts. The kids will pore over the catalog, making their choices. Brainstorm also offers surprise gift packs (like grab bags) put together at a nice savings. All can be delivered before New Year's Day.

• Gifts from your own belongings. Look through your belongings—all the things that have accumulated through the years and you no longer have a use for in your life. Anything you don't want or use anymore can be a thrilling gift for a kid. There may be drawers and closets full of things imaginative or fashion-conscious nine-year-olds would like— scarfs, fabrics, hats, costume jewelry. Pack it all in an old small suitcase, decorative box, or trunk. Affix a small mirror inside the suitcase or box lid and voilà!, you've made a portable dressing room/fashion studio. They will make costumes, outfits for play, "dress-up" as we used to call it; perhaps create a real wardrobe. Hide a gift inside, too—a new doll, a sewing kit, a book or toy.

For kids with more outdoorsy tastes, fill a trunk or backpack with adventure or fix-it supplies that you've gathered from your own things—old watch, pocket knife, compass, magnifying glass, canteen, maps, small light-activated calculator, fishing vest, flashlight, key chain, belt, hat. Hide a gift in there, too—a harmonica, an adventure video, or a Hardy Boys story.

GIFT IDEAS
FOR LOVED ONES AND
FRIENDS

Handmade Gifts

There is nothing more personal than a gift that has been
planned and made by hand. Here are a few ideas.

Theme Calendars

This is a great family project. Working on it a little every
day provides quality time together and a focus for your
youngsters' (or your own) excitement.

Buy a 9- × 12-inch sketch pad with spiral binding,
which you can find in a stationery or art supply store.
Choose one with the fewest number of pages—under fifty
is best.

You will also need a glue stick, small hole-punch, and
fine-point and medium-point felt-tip markers; plus optional decorative rubber stamps, stickers, crayons, and the
like.

Position the pad so that it opens to the 12-inch
width. To make it a hanging calendar, measure first then
punch a small hole in the center bottom of each page,
about one-half inch from the bottom border. Decorate
the top page, write down the name of the month, and
draw a grid of squares for the month on the bottom page.

With a glue stick, glue the back of the month-grid
page to the face of the next page. Eventually this process

will make each month page and decorated page double thickness.

Now choose a theme for the calendar: If it's a gift for Dad, each month's decoration can be about something that he likes or enjoys doing, the things he has accomplished or still dreams about doing. Include photos and quotations (things he's noted for saying), photos of family reunions, pictures cut out from magazines of places he'd like to go, letters from the kids, photo collages of him in different moods and poses.

Each family member could add a drawing or painting each month. Kids can cut words out of magazines and paste them on specific days—"DAD" on Father's Day, for example.

Work on the calendar a little bit every day. If the

sketch pad is big enough, you will have room left over for a calendar next year, too. Some sketch pads hold three years' worth of calendars, which make wonderful keepsakes.

Memory Box
Decorate a cigar box by gluing a collage of hand-printed literary quotes, pieces of fabric, theater stubs, photos, pieces of high school programs, mementos of events through the year. Cover each section—top, sides, and bottom—with clear self-adhesive paper.

Frame Anything
Have your child make a drawing . . . and frame it for her grandparents.

Make a memory collage much like a memory box for your girlfriend with mementos such as photos, postcards from vacations, the movie stub from your first date, the program from college commencement, childhood photos, and frame it.

If your brother is devoted to his dog, make a collage of photos of the dog with famous quotes about dogs and frame it.

❧

Christmas Crafts

Handmade wreaths, ornaments, and other Christmas decorations make excellent gifts. (See p. 119.)

❧

Hand-lettered, or Computer-designed "Certificates of Comfort and Joy"

These certificates promise time, energy, and devotion for the well-being of the lucky recipient. Here are some of my favorites:

- Massage (six one-hour sessions)
- Travel (one weekend in the mountains, or on a boat, or camping, or at a luxury hotel)
- Adventure (one flight soaring in a glider or in a balloon, or one bungee-jump)
- Time out for lunch and conversation (one Tuesday every month)
- Car wash (one a month for . . .)
- Dog walking (every day for . . .)
- Furniture shopping

Kitchen-made Gifts

Those once-a-year food gifts of jams, jellies, and sauces in jars with homemade labels, and cookies and candy in bright colored tins and boxes, glazed nuts layered in large glass jars, soup mixes, herbs and spices, and jars of homemade mustard and chutneys are welcome at my house and appreciated when I bring them to others. For recipes, see p. 103.

Found Treasures—Great Gifts

All kinds of presents are waiting to be discovered in the most unlikely places—flea markets or swap meets, church rummage sales, yard sales, used book and used clothing stores. Old finds can become new treasures with a little personal touch.

A friend once gave me a slightly battered copy of *Glinda of Oz*, one of the original Oz books, that she'd found at a flea market. I loved it. What lessened its value to a collector made it priceless to me. The original owner, a little girl by the name of Rosalyn, had drawn on the title page a hieroglyphic attempt at her name!

Old cookbooks make great presents for cooking enthusiasts. Pack one in an antique mixing bowl with an assortment of spices, a new pepper grinder, and a wire whisk. Wrap it all in cellophane and a grosgrain ribbon bow.

First-edition novels can be treasures for the avid reader or collector. Rare books don't have to be expensive, either. I once found the first ever James Taylor songbook for only $2. Of course, that went to a Taylor fan along with his latest CD.

Wooden boxes, trunks, Victorian hat boxes, antique postcards and posters, retro clothing and jewelry, outdated kitchen utensils, ceramic pitchers and dinner plates all make wonderful gifts, containers for gifts, or enhancements to gift wrappings.

What to Do with What You Find

A small ceramic pitcher can be filled with fresh juniper greens and small bright ornaments or bunches of dried bay leaves, rosemary, and thyme tied with a ribbon.

Also, classic diner plates at $1 each are great for giving Christmas cookies and are much more interesting than paper plates.

When filled with red and green Christmas candy or chocolate kisses and wrapped with cellophane and ribbon, those bright colored aluminum tumblers I grew up with in the '50s make a wonderful treat for a fellow baby boomer.

Fill antique bottles with dried flowers.

Antique or Deco and '50s' picture frames make fine gifts by themselves, or use them to frame the photo of the latest family reunion. Less special frames can be sprayed gold or covered with self-adhesive paper or fabric.

Old ceramic bowls or large canning jars are nifty when you fill them with homemade cookies or other goodies.

A ceramic or brass flower pot or wicker plant stand might look great with gardening goods in it—gloves, spades, seeds for spring, and a great green bow.

A good-looking basket is a fine container for gourmet condiments—mustard, chutney, tapinade, curry, rice. Or fill it with a packet of biscotti, a tin of tea, a bag of coffee. Or with soaps, lotions, bubble bath—and a good book to read while soaking.

An old leather satchel or book bag can be filled with supplies for the art student—pens, brushes, sketch pads.

For collectors, you might find something they would

love to add to their collection, but then add your own personal touch. For example:

> To the teacup and saucer, attach a printed card with a date for afternoon tea
>
> To the teaspoon, attach a date for lunch
>
> To the antique stuffed animal, attach tickets to see *Cats* or a date to go to the zoo or the aquarium
>
> To the antique book, include a gift certificate to a bookstore
>
> Into the antique cookie jar, add homemade cookies and your recipe

GIFT GIVING FOR COUPLES

Here are a few warnings and suggestions garnered from my interviews with young and old couples, as well as from my own life experience.

- Know your partner's size—carry dress size, shirt, blouse, pants, and shoe sizes on a card in your purse or wallet. Keep track of sizes if they go up or down.
- Don't give gifts that he or she is trying to avoid. For the partner trying to diet, avoid chocolate truffles. If he or she has said, "No more mystery books, I'm becoming addicted to them," then give a classic novel instead.

- Don't give gift certificates or cash. These are highly impersonal and unromantic.
- Don't give what you've decided is for your partner's own good—such as self-help books, Thigh Masters, or Belly-Begones.
- Don't give hint gifts hoping that your partner will catch on—home repair books and tool boxes for the one you would like to work more around the house; cookbooks for the one you'd like to cook more; gym memberships for . . .
- Don't give joke gifts. If he doesn't like flashy underwear, don't get him the purple silk briefs—not for Christmas, anyway.
- Don't give him or her something that's really for the house—new gutters, front door, garage door opener, dishwasher. Buy these things in the spring, summer, or fall, not Christmas.
- Don't consider a heavy appliance a personal gift. If you really want to give him or her a new washer and dryer, make it secondary to the beautifully wrapped box with a cashmere sweater inside that's sitting on top of it.
- If you want to give an appliance, such as a vibrator for muscle massage, then include a nice bottle of massage oil and a hand-lettered certificate good for so many massages from you or a gift certificate for a professional massage at the spa.
- If you're going to give a phone, for instance, a cellular phone, then make it as personal as you can. Have it charged up and ready to use. Arrange for your

partner's best friend to call the new phone at a certain hour.

- Give any piece of jewelry as long as it's real gold or silver, pearls, or gemstones.
- Give sports memorabilia or equipment, team jackets, tickets to sporting events.
- Give a trip to the spa for massage and sauna followed by a cozy dinner and concert tickets.
- Listen to your partner for clues and give anything that has been mentioned repeatedly. Examples might include:
  I love those plush bathrobes you get in four-star hotels.
  I have yet to see a Knicks game live—I just can't manage to order before the tickets sell out.
  I'd love to go to D.C. to see the cherry blossoms.
- Don't give gifts that *you* really want. If your partner is less adventurous/sporty than you, he or she won't enjoy books, videos, or calendars from *National Geographic*, no matter how beautiful they are. Nor will he or she really want a new wind-surfing board!
- Make gifts personal and special to Christmas. Let your gifts indulge your partner. For example, if your partner enjoys a fine cigar, he or she probably will appreciate a box of them even if smoking has been banned from the house.
- Give any gift of travel—vouchers good for one trip anywhere, train tickets, ski-lift tickets, a hotel room key and reservations, reservations at a lovely bed and breakfast, cruise tickets . . .

SHOPPING TIPS

So, you are ready with a gift list. Before you head out on the hunt, think about what kind of shopper you are and plan accordingly. Some people can shop all day long. Others are ready to collapse into a fatigued dementia after two hours. If you are someone who runs out of energy quickly, then spread your shopping tasks over a couple days or even a week.

Always try to go shopping when you are at your best. If you're a night person, plenty of places are open late—some even round the clock. If you're a morning person, by all means go early. Ginny Folan, my contributor in Santa Barbara, is at the mall at 6:00 A.M., when it opens. She schedules in lunch and lots of coffee breaks and does almost all her shopping in one day.

Before you leave the house, map out your shopping stops in a way that will maximize convenience and efficiency. For example, start farthest from home and work back. Or use your own energy as a priority and shop at self-service stores first when you are fresh, and save the stores noted for good service for the end, when you will need the TLC.

Try not to combine gift shopping with grocery shopping or any other kind of errands—doing so tends to split your focus and tire you. Of course, if you happen to see something for yourself as you are picking out a gift for someone else, go ahead and buy it, but don't plan any other such tasks when you are gift shopping.

It's ideal to wrap gifts, tag them, and put them in a special closet or hideaway on the day you buy them. If you can't manage the wrapping just then, be sure to mark the boxes clearly before you hide them away.

Special Shop Stops

If you aren't already involved with a church or charity organization, call the ones in your area and find out which sponsor craft and/or bake fairs. Bake fairs in particular are a boon to Sharon Kopenski, my contributor in Madison, Wisconsin. Sharon shops every year at the local church Cookie Walk (a bake fair) benefit. For $20 she can buy pounds of beautifully decorated cookies—more than she needs for at-home entertaining and for gifts for neighbors and friends.

Local craft fairs offer unique handmade wreaths, candles, centerpieces, stockings, and ornaments to use, give away, or add as decoration to packages.

When you're looking for something extra—that second gift or stocking stuffer—plan stops at special shops, such as the gift shop at the folk art museum, modern art museum, zoo, and science and nature museum. There you will find wonderful gifts such as handmade puppets, posters, or books for science lovers.

Art supply stores are a good source for the young and budding or full-blown artist. Sketch pads, pastels, and watercolors are terrific Christmas gifts.

KIDS SHOP, TOO

Plan a special time to take your children shopping, when you don't have to focus on doing your own. When I was growing up, my mom gave my three brothers and me $5 each and took us to the local J.J. Newberry store. She waited in the car for thirty minutes while we bought our Christmas surprises. Inside the store, we separated and often dodged out of sight of each other in order to keep our buys a secret. In those days, the Newberry aisles were rows of wooden bins, piled high with all kinds of un-wrapped goods, from toys and tools to socks, reading glasses, and lingerie. It was a hands-on shopping spree that often took longer than the allotted time.

I still remember those gifts—small bottles of toilet water or soap for my mother, some kind of screwdriver or a handkerchief or foot powder for Dad. For one another, there were magnifying glasses, small number-moving puz-zles, rabbit's foot key chains, pick-up-sticks, a deck of cards, rubber pirate's daggers, whistles, harmonicas, cray-ons, coloring books.

Nowadays, take older kids (young teens) to the mall and plan to meet back at a restaurant in an hour. If you have younger kids, you should accompany them on their shopping trip. Perhaps you and another mom or dad can switch kids for a shopping hour. Remain close at hand as your friend's kids shop for presents, and promise not to divulge their surprises.

SHOPPING BY PHONE

Many Americans shop by phone on a regular basis. Something like 12 billion catalogs are delivered to us each year. Ten thousand companies with catalogs make a total of more than $60 billion every year.

Here is a list of some of the merchandise that is available from catalogs. Call the companies in September for catalogs or information. Most companies mail their catalogs third class, and they can take a month to reach you. Remember, the earlier you order from the catalog, the more likely you are to find the style, size, or color of what you want in stock.

If you subscribe to an online computer service, such as CompuServe, Prodigy, or America On Line, you will find the same shopping convenience but without the catalogs.

Christmas Greenery

Mt. Rainier Greenery in Washington State offers beautiful 22-inch fresh balsam fir wreaths. Call 1-800-862-6000. Also 1-800-Flowers has a great reputation for delivering fresh Christmas arrangements on time.

Personal Gifts

The Memories Calendar. For about $25, these folks will enlarge twelve photos you submit and return them to you with a large picture calendar featuring your photos (one for every month). Call 1-800-821-0012.

Food

American Spoon Foods offers wonderful jams, jellies, preserves, and nuts. Call 1-800-222-5886.

The Chocolate Club will send a new assortment of chocolate every month. Call 1-800-901-9910.

Ducktrap River Fish Farm in Maine offers smoked fish. Call 1-800-828-3825.

The Dulin Brothers, Kansas City Steaks, deliver steaks. Call 1-800-893-8844.

Fiddler on the Green in Maine sells breakfast baskets full of organic jams, syrups, honey, and mixes for scones and pancakes. Call 1-800-729-7935.

Grace Woods Groves in Vero Beach, Florida, offers a half bushel of Indian River grapefruit and honey in a big beautiful gift box for under $20. Call 1-800-678-1154.

Harrington Vermont offers smoked ham or cob-smoked turkey breast. Call 1-802-434-4444.

Harry and David, originators of the Fruit of the Month Club, also offer fruitcake, baby vegetables, and pumpkin cheesecake. Call 1-800-842-6111.

Lake Champlain Chocolates will send two truffles with their catalog. Call 1-800-464-5909.

New Penny Farm in Presque Isle, Maine, offers a Potato of the Month. Call 1-800-827-7551.

Ozark Mountains Smokehouse sells smoked hams and turkeys, and green tomato pickles. Call 1-800-643-3437.

Omaha Steaks. Call 1-800-228-9055.

Sarabeth's Kitchen in New York City makes brownies and cranberry relish. Call 1-800-552-5267.

Stag's Leap Winery sells fine California wines. Call 1-800-640-5327.

The Trappist Monastery offers Monastery Country Cheese that is fine and creamy. To establish contact write 3365 Monastery Drive, Crozet, VA 22932.

The Vermont Country Store offers maple-sugar candies, crackers, canned Indian pudding, and more. Call 1-802-362-2400.

Wolferman's sells giant English muffins. Call 1-800-999-0169.

Clothes and Comfort

Ebbets Field Flannels offers replica classic baseball jerseys, jackets, and caps from the minor and Negro leagues. Call 1-800-377-9777.

J. Crew sells jackets, sweaters, pants and T-shirts for men and women. Call 1-800-562-0258.

Lands End Direct Merchants offers rugged, warm, and practical clothing for men, women and children. Call 1-800-356-4444.

Tilley Endurables sells travel clothes, including the Tilley hat. Call 1-800-884-7171.

Victoria's Secret sells beautiful lingerie. Call 1-800-888-8200.

Adult and Kids' Toys

Brainstorm sells gadgets, fun items, and science toys mostly for kids. Call 1-800-621-7500.

Childcraft, Inc., sells toys for kids. Call 1-800-631-5657.

Hammacher Schlemmer offers gadgets and terrifically eccentric inventions. Call 1-800-233-4800.

Toys to Grow On sells toys for eighteen months and up. Call 1-800-542-8338.

Computers, Software, and Electronics

Mac Warehouse. Call 1-800-255-6227.

PC Connection sells software, including CD/ROMs. Call 1-800-800-0005.

Cooks and Kitchen

The Chef's Catalog offers tools for kitchen utility and food preparation. Call 1-800-338-3232.

Pottery Barn sells items for kitchen and home. Call 1-800-922-5507.

Williams-Sonoma, famed outfitters for the home cook. Call 1-800-541-2233.

Garden Accessories

Burpee sells garden seeds. Call 1-800-888-1447.

Smith and Hawken in California sells bulbs, furniture, equipment, tools, and clothing. Call 1-415-383-7030.

Books and Videos

BookBound offers any book in print. Call 1-800-959-read.

Books on Tape, in Newport Beach, California. Call 1-800-626-3333.

Critics Choice Video. Call 1-800-367-7765.

Special Gifts

Art Matters sells wonderful pieces direct from the artists to you; proceeds go to support the arts. Call 1-800-909-7656.

Body Shop offers fine, politically correct skin care products, produced without testing on animals, interfering with the health of the rain forest, or exploiting native populations. Call 1-800-541-2535.

The Metropolitan Museum of Art is the place for classic posters, reprints, and replicas of antique jewelry. Call 1-800-369-7386.

Stave Jigsaw Puzzles offers beautiful hand-cut, expensive wooden jigsaw puzzles. Call 1-802-295-5200.

Tiffany & Co. has some affordable goods with the famous name, including pens, key chains, stationery. Call 1-800-526-0649.

For $300 you can have an artist do a pen-and-ink drawing of your home or some other landmark near and dear to you. Call 1-206-746-2981.

WRAPPING IT UP

Wrapping the gift is as much a personal statement as choosing it. Be prepared.

Make a run for paper, cellophane, wire ribbon, fabric, bows, tissue paper, tape, and tags before you begin your gift shopping. Make room for it all in one corner, closet, basement, or attic. If your home has limited space, empty a drawer for the season, or buy a tall kitchen wastebasket to hold all your rolls of paper. Keep tape, scissors, tags, and small ornaments for wrapping in a separate shoe box.

Special Wraps

I have several friends who save anything they think might make a unique or meaningful gift wrap. At various times they've used wallpaper from the children's rooms for their now-grown children, special front-page headlines for the history buff, sports pages for the hockey or baseball fan, comics for the humor fan, swatches of burlap or fabric from home-sewn clothes, place mats from landmark hotels, shopping bags with familiar logos, old sheet music or movie posters for old-movie fans, and maps of foreign cities and American towns for travelers.

Two-Minute Wrap

Using a glue stick, make a swirl design on the outside of a small brown paper lunch bag and sprinkle the design with glitter. Press the glitter down lightly, then brush off any remaining loose glitter.

Wrap the gift loosely in colorful tissue and place it in the paper bag. Fluff the tissue out the top, and sprinkle glitter over the top of the tissue.

Proxy Wrap

If you run out of time, remember there are dozens of services now that will wrap and ship packages for you—and dozens of neighborhood teenagers looking to make extra money at Christmas.

MAILING AND SHIPPING

For US domestic first-class postage, mail packages no later
than December 15. Of course it's possible to mail later
and pay extra priority delivery charges.

For UPS (800-742-5877) and FedEx (800-463-3339),
call the day before you want your packages picked up.

Checklist for Gift Giving

November 1–8
☆   Make general gift lists.

November 8–15
☆   Shop for gifts on your list.

☆   Gather material for handmade gift projects.

☆   Buy wrapping supplies—paper, wire ribbon, bows,
tape, tags, bags, tissue paper, cellophane . . .

November 16–21
☆   Buy ingredients and materials for homemade gifts.

☆   Begin handmade gift projects. (See p. 119.)

❦

November 22–30

☆   If you haven't done so already, order gifts from catalogs.

☆   Start Christmas baking and freeze for later use.

☆   Wrap and mail gifts for out-of-country delivery.

❦

December 1–8

☆   Make wish lists with the younger children.

☆   Complete handmade craft projects.

☆   Complete Christmas baking and freeze for later use. Include gingerbread cookie ornaments to be used later. (See p. 135.)

❦

December 9–15

☆   Wrap all remaining gifts. Mail or ship any for domestic delivery.

☆   Buy any last-minute gifts and stocking stuffers.

❄️

December 16–22
☆   Deliver gifts to friends and co-workers.

GIFTS FROM THE KITCHEN

Here are recipes for a few delectable cookies, candy, jams, and chutneys. Wrap the cookies in cellophane, pack them into bright tins, or heap them onto gift platters or into colorful baskets with jars of jams and spicy chutneys.

Sharon Kopenski's Bourbon Balls

These are easy-to-make classic Christmas sweets. Sharon uses a salad shooter to crush her vanilla wafers. I use the blender on "crush" for 10 seconds.

6 ounces chocolate morsels
1 cup confectioner's sugar, plus extra for rolling
1/3 cup evaporated milk
1/3 cup bourbon (or rum, or brandy)
2 cup vanilla wafers crumbs
1/2 cup chopped pecans

Melt the chocolate in the top of a double boiler over hot but not boiling water until smooth. Cool slightly.

In a mixing bowl, combine the chocolate and the confectioner's sugar and stir until blended. Add the evaporated milk, bourbon, wafers and nuts and stir until a stiff batter forms. Shape into 1-inch balls and roll the balls in confectioner's sugar. Place in a covered container between layers of waxed paper and keep in a cool place.

MAKES ABOUT 4 DOZEN.

Chad's Favorite Chocolate-Peanut Butter Bonbons

These are such a favorite in the Kopenski house that Sharon used to have to hide them from her son, Chad, who would devour them all before the holiday. Sharon makes a double batch nowadays just to make sure they'll last.

2 cups confectioner's sugar
1/2 cup chocolate wafer crumbs
1/2 cup graham cracker crumbs
3/4 cup chopped hazelnuts or pecans
1/2 cup flaked coconut
1/2 cup (1 stick) butter or margarine
1/2 cup smooth peanut butter
1/2 cup semisweet chocolate morsels
3 tablespoons margarine

In a large bowl, combine the confectioner's sugar, wafer and cracker crumbs, nuts, and coconut. In a small saucepan, melt the butter and peanut butter until smooth; stir into crumb mixture until well moistened. Shape the mixture into 1-inch balls.

Melt the chocolate and margarine in the top of a double boiler over hot but not boiling water until smooth. Cool slightly. Roll each ball in the chocolate mixture until well coated. Using a wooden pick, spear each ball and place on waxed paper. Chill well before storing.

Place the chilled bonbons in a covered container between layers of waxed paper and store in a cool place.

MAKES 4 DOZEN.

Rocky Road Bars

These rich three-layer chocolate nut bars are well worth the time it takes to make them.

Preheat the oven to 350°F. Grease and flour a 9- × 13-inch pan.

FOR THE COOKIE BASE:
1/2 cup butter or margarine
1 ounce unsweetened chocolate
1 cup granulated sugar
1 egg
1 teaspoon vanilla
1 cup all-purpose flour
1 teaspoon baking powder
1/2 cup chopped walnuts

Melt the butter and unsweetened chocolate in a small saucepan over hot but not boiling water until smooth. Cool slightly.

In a large bowl, combine the sugar, egg, vanilla, flour, baking powder, and nuts. Stir in the chocolate until well blended. Spread evenly in prepared pan.

FOR THE FILLING:

6 ounces cream cheese
1/2 cup granulated sugar
1/4 cup butter, softened
1 egg
2 tablespoons all-purpose flour
1/2 teaspoon vanilla
1/4 cup chopped walnuts
6 ounces semisweet chocolate morsels
2 cups miniature marshmallows

In a large bowl, combine the cream cheese, sugar, butter, and egg and beat until smooth. Add the flour and vanilla and continue beating until fluffy. Stir in the nuts until well blended. Spread filling over cookie mixture in the pan. Sprinkle with chocolate chips. Bake until firm, 25 to 30 minutes. Sprinkle evenly with marshmallows and bake 2 minutes longer.

FOR THE FROSTING:

2 ounces cream cheese
1 ounce unsweetened chocolate
1/4 cup butter
1/4 cup milk
1 teaspoon vanilla
3 cups confectioner's sugar

In a saucepan, melt the cream cheese, chocolate, butter, milk, and vanilla until smooth. Add the confectioner's sugar and stir until smooth. Cool slightly.

When the marshmallows are just melted on top of the filling, spread evenly with frosting and swirl. Refrigerate until well cooled. Cut into approximately 2¼-inch squares and store in between layers of waxed paper in a tightly covered container in a cool place.

MAKES 24 BARS.

Nana Folan's Crescents

Ginny Folan's mother-in-law has been making these every holiday for as long as Ginny has known her.

1 cup (2 sticks) butter or margarine, softened
¼ cup granulated sugar
2 cups all-purpose flour
1 cup ground unblanched almonds
1 teaspoon vanilla
Confectioner's sugar

Heat the oven to 300°F. Lightly grease a cookie sheet.

In a large bowl, beat the butter and sugar until light. Add the flour, almonds, and vanilla and stir until blended.

Shape small amounts of the dough into crescents about 3 inches by 1 inch by ½-inch thick. Dredge in confectioner's sugar and place on a cookie sheet. Bake 35 minutes.

Cool completely on a rack, then dredge each in confectioner's sugar again. Store between layers of waxed paper in a tightly covered container in a cool place.

MAKES 3 DOZEN.

Mrs. Petrini's Sugar Cookies

A favorite neighbor to Ginny Folan when she was growing up, Mrs. Petrini has treated her own children, several grandchildren, church groups, and neighbors to these delectables.

2 eggs, lightly beaten
1 cup granulated sugar
1 cup confectioner's sugar
1 cup vegetable oil
1 cup vegetable shortening
5 cups all-purpose flour
1½ teaspoons baking soda
1 teaspoon cream of tartar
1½ teaspoons salt
Red or green sugar crystals

Heat the oven to 350°F.

In a large bowl, combine the eggs, sugars, oil, and short-ening, and beat until smooth. Stir in the flour, baking soda, cream of tartar, and salt until well combined. Roll dough into 1-inch balls and place on an ungreased cookie sheet. Flatten with the bottom of a glass. Sprinkle with colored sugar and bake for 12 to 15 minutes.

Cool completely on a rack and store between layers of waxed paper in a tightly covered container in a cool place.

MAKES 5 DOZEN.

Hazelnut Biscotti

This classic twice-baked cookie is popular with cappuccino lovers.

1 1/2 cups all-purpose flour
1/2 teaspoon baking powder
1/3 cup shelled hazelnuts, coarsely chopped
4 egg whites
1 egg
3/4 cup granulated sugar
1 teaspoon vanilla

Preheat the oven to 350°F. Lightly grease 2 baking sheets. In a small bowl, combine the flour, baking powder, and hazelnuts. In a large bowl, beat the egg whites and egg until frothy. Gradually beat in the sugar and vanilla until thick. Fold the flour mixture into the egg mixture just until well combined.

Spoon half the batter into a 12- × 4-inch strip on one baking sheet; repeat with the remaining batter on the other baking sheet. The batter will spread slightly.

Bake the strips until golden brown, about 20 minutes. Cool on the baking sheets on wire racks for 10 minutes. Remove the strips from the baking sheets and cut crosswise into 1/2-inch-thick slices. Place a single layer of biscotti cut side down on a baking sheet and bake 10 to 15 minutes longer, turning the slices halfway through baking until light and golden brown on both sides. Cool completely on baking sheets on wire racks. Store between layers of waxed paper in a tightly covered tin.

MAKES ABOUT **40** BISCOTTI.

Tom's Christmas Candy

The best almond brittle candy and so easy to make. Tom Folan makes it every year. Now you can, too.

1 ounce semisweet or milk chocolate, shaved
2 cups finely chopped walnuts
1 pound (4 sticks) butter
2 cups granulated sugar
2 cups whole almonds

Grease a baking sheet and line it with aluminum foil. Combine the chocolate and the walnuts and spread half the chocolate mixture over the baking sheet.

In a saucepan, combine the butter, sugar, and almonds. Cook over medium-high heat, stirring constantly, until candy thermometer registers 310°F. Pour this mixture over the chocolate mixture on the baking sheet. Top with remaining chocolate mixture and cool completely. Break into serving-size pieces and store between layers of waxed paper in a tightly covered tin in a cool place.

MAKES ABOUT 2 POUNDS

Cranberries in Grand Marnier

Among the sweetest accompaniments the late Bert Greene ever gave me or taught me to make, this one is my favorite.

1 cup orange juice
2 cups granulated sugar
1 pound cranberries (4 cups), washed and picked over
Flesh of 1 orange, all pith removed, seeded and chopped
2 tablespoons finely slivered orange rind
½ cup Grand Marnier

In a large saucepan combine the orange juice and sugar. Cook, stirring, over medium heat until the sugar dissolves. Add the cranberries, orange flesh, and orange rind. Heat to boiling and reduce the heat; simmer until the cranberry skins pop and cranberries are tender, about 10 minutes. Add the Grand Marnier and simmer 5 minutes longer. Pour into hot sterilized jars. Seal and store in the refrigerator.

MAKES 3 PINTS.

Apple Christmas Relish

Here's a terrific accompaniment for smoked meats that makes a much-appreciated gift.

2 Granny Smith apples, peeled, cored, and quartered
Juice of 1 lemon
Slivered rind of 1 lemon
Juice and pulp of 1 orange
Slivered rind of 1 orange
12-ounce package cranberries, washed and picked over
1 cup superfine sugar
$^1/_4$ cup apple brandy (optional)

Place the apples in the container of a food processor or blender. Add lemon juice, lemon peel, orange juice and pulp, and orange peel. Pulse on and off until finely chopped. Transfer to a large bowl.

Place the cranberries in the container of a food processor or blender. Add the sugar and brandy, if desired, and process until finely chopped. Combine the cranberries and apple mixture in a mixing bowl until mixed thoroughly. Spoon into sterilized jars. Store in the refrigerator for up to 4 weeks.

MAKES ABOUT 2 PINTS.

Christmas Raspberry Jam

According to Ginny Folan, this is the homemade food that pleases all the relatives. She makes batches and batches of it at Christmas only. If she skips a year, the relatives complain.

2 cups fresh raspberries, mashed
2 cups granulated sugar
Juice of ½ lemon

Cook the berries in a medium saucepan over low heat for 30 minutes. Add ½ cup sugar and bring to a boil. Add the lemon juice alternating with the remaining sugar, returning the berries to a boil after each addition. Cook until jam has thickened. Ladle into sterilized jars and seal. Store in a cool place.

MAKES ABOUT 3 PINTS.

Spirited Fruit Chutney

Make this to accompany smoked and spicy meat.

1/2 pineapple, peeled, cored, cut into 1 1/4-inch chunks (about 1 3/4
     cups)
2 pears, peeled, cored, and sliced
1 small mango (about 6 ounces)
Pulp from 1/2 large orange
1/4 cup orange juice
3/4 cup dark brown sugar, packed
4 ounces dried figs, cut into pieces
1/4 cup dark raisins
4 dried apricots
Finely slivered rind from 1/2 lemon
Finely slivered rind from 1/2 orange
1 1/2 teaspoons candied ginger, cut into strips
1/2 teaspoon ground mace
1 cinnamon stick broken in half
3/4 cup walnut meats
1/2 cup grated coconut
1 1/2 teaspoons white vinegar
3/4 cup dark rum

In a medium saucepan combine the fresh fruits, juice, and sugar. Heat to boiling, reduce the heat, and simmer 5 minutes. Add the dried fruits, lemon and orange rinds, candied ginger, mace, and cinnamon. Simmer 30 minutes. Add the walnuts, coconut, and vinegar. Continue to cook until all the fruit is soft. Add the rum and bring the mixture to just under a boil. Remove from the heat. Spoon into hot sterilized jars, seal, and store in a cool place for up to several months.

MAKES ABOUT 2 PINTS.

SUCCESS TIPS
FOR COOKIE GIFTS

- Use the kind of fat called for in the recipe—oil, shortening, butter, or margarine. If butter or margarine is called for, use it in stick form. The same amount in whipped form or spreads contains more water and less fat, and will affect results.
- For making cookies with kids, choose simple one-bowl recipes. Make extra, even double batches, because kids make mistakes. They also eat as much dough as they bake. Little kids should use sturdy spoons that are easy to hold.
- Freeze cookies up to 2 months. Once thawed, almost any cookie tastes as good as fresh. Be sure cookies are completely cooled before freezing. Place them in heavy-duty plastic freezer bags or between layers of waxed paper in airtight containers.

  Thaw cookies in their containers for 2 hours, or remove them and let them stand at room temperature for 30 minutes. If cookies are supposed to be crisp, refresh them by placing them in the oven at 300°F for about 5 minutes.

- For big batches, use two baking sheets and aluminum foil that has been cut to fit the baking sheets. While one batch of cookies is baking, ready the next batch on the foil. When you remove one batch from the oven, place the foil filled with unbaked cookies on the baking sheets.
- To keep cookies crisp, pack them in airtight containers. They'll stay crisp for about a week. If they do become soggy, recrisp them in a 300°F oven for 5 minutes.

CHAPTER VIII
The Handmade Christmas

Making a fresh evergreen wreath, designing your own greeting card, creating a new ornament or gingerbread house, carrying home and trimming the tree, and wrapping packages with hand-tied bows brings a personal character to your Christmas that touches all those around you and remains uniquely yours in memory.

Make it a point to give yourself a little time to make something this Christmas. Something as simple as stringing popcorn or cranberries for the tree while listening to music, sipping hot cider, and chatting with others calms the mind, pleases the soul, invites the Christmas spirit in, and, more important, creates moments you don't ever forget.

Craft magazines and the special holiday editions of magazines such as *Ladies' Home Journal*, *Good Housekeeping* and *McCall's* are jam-packed with inspiration for a vast array of exciting projects—from easy-to-make ornaments, candle holders, stockings, personalized greeting cards, and wrappings, to elaborate quilts and tapestries.

My longtime friend Ginny Folan is a devout handmade Christmas aficionada. Around mid-September she starts meeting weekly with a group of friends to make ornaments, the ideas for which come from magazines.

My neighbor Barbara McTiernan has done the same, amassing hundreds of original ornaments and craft pieces over the years. Both she and Ginny tell me that there are three secrets to getting projects completed:

- A passion for a homemade personal atmosphere in the home at Christmas
- A plan
- A glue gun

The rest is easy; with a few materials and not much time, anyone can turn out bushy fragrant wreaths, original greeting cards, ornaments, and much much more.

GETTING CRAFT PROJECTS OFF THE GROUND AND COMPLETED

1. Get started early—late November is okay, early November is better. Choose one or two simple projects to accomplish on your own or with others.
2. Use your local copy/print shop for help with handmade greeting cards.
3. Locate your nearest floral or crafts supply store, home decorations store, and fabric shop. This is where you will buy circular wreath forms, Styrofoam forms, floral wire, ornament hooks, and decorative touches, such as bunches of faux berries, millinery fruit and tiny pinecones, miniature snowmen, Santas,

white glue, a glue gun, spray paint, ornament
hangers, and silver and gold thread.

4. Spread the projects out over a few days, writing your start and finish dates on the calendar.
Begin making Earth Angel ornaments one day,
for example, and spray paint them on another.
Or bake the gingerbread ornaments one day
and assemble and decorate on another day.

5. Set aside a space that can remain messy until
projects are complete.

CHRISTMAS CARDS

Handmade cards are the most pleasurable for me to receive and send. Friends and relatives send me Christmas
letters with hand-drawn designs between paragraphs and
in the margins, handwritten (albeit photocopied) letters
tucked inside store-bought cards, and home-designed
cards, complete with original drawings and verse.

The Christmas Letter

Lots of personal details is the key to a good Christmas
letter. Try to keep it to one or two $8\frac{1}{2}$- × 11-inch pages
typed or written, while leaving room between paragraphs,
in the middle of sentences, and in margins for added
designs and decoration.

   To decorate the letter, use rubber stamps to fill the
spaces on the page, or use drawings by the kids, words or

designs you've cut from magazine layouts and pasted down, even parts of photographs.

Take the completed letter design to a print/copy shop and have as many as you want printed on colored paper.

One Christmas, a writer I know detailed in typed single-spaced hilarity her cross-country assignments from the previous year. To illustrate the bizarreness of her travel-assignment schedule, she took pictures of herself in a photo booth at Woolworth's, quickly changing baseball-style caps from the different places she'd written about through the year: Toledo Mud Hens, Planet Hollywood, Anchorage Truck & Salvage, Peoria Caterpillar Expo, Rock & Roll Hall of Fame, California Whale Watch, Disneyworld, and finally Connecticut Pork Farmers.

She then cut each photo from the strips and pasted them here and there throughout the letter.

Greeting Cards

Handmade greeting cards are easy to produce these days. Anyone with a computer and printer with graphics capability can design a layout, scan and include photographs, and typeset a personal message in very little time. When the design is completed and printed out, all you have to do is take it to a print shop, of which there seem to be as many of as convenience stores, and have the artwork printed on card stock (heavy-weight paper) to fit stock size envelopes. Your computer also can produce mailing labels.

The photo card is one of the easiest and most personal handmade cards to do without a computer. Choose a photo you'd like to use to say happy holidays—a family gathering, you at work or play, or a special nature scene. My nephew Paul once sent one of his dog, Montana, wearing reindeer antlers. Take the photo to a photo shop and have it printed as a postcard. Then you can add your message to the back with the address and mail it as a postcard, or you can place it in an envelope.

For the past ten years, Ginny and Tom Folan and their sons Michael and Kevin have sent me a printed, hand-drawn card with original verse. Tom or Ginny takes the artwork to the local copy/print shop and *voilá!* One hundred cards on any color card stock they want. I have kept all of them. My favorite is one with a stick drawing of a shepherd and lamb looking up at a star, with the words:

> In the middle of the night,
> The shepherds saw the special light.
> A newborn babe brought peace and hope
> and gave us directions on how to cope.

Inside the card read:

> We wish you glee as you trim your tree
> and we hope you cope in '93!

Last Christmas my friend Catherine Schurdack came up with an easy-to-make card with a simple and elegant design. It didn't involve a print shop, photo shop, or computer.

Start with a stack of white or cream-colored 4- × 6-inch card stock. (You can buy it at an office, statio-

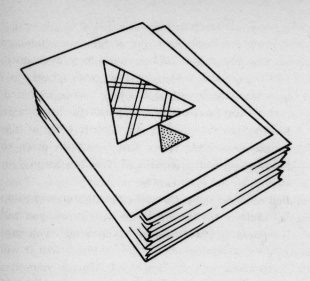

nery, or printer supply store.) Buy envelopes, too. In a housewares or hardware shop, buy a roll of colorful luminescent self-adhesive shelf paper—bright green, gold, plaid. Now all you need is a good pair of scissors or X-acto knife, a pen and ruler, and a flat place to work.

Unroll the paper so that it is lying flat—use a heavy object on the corner if needed. Using a pen and ruler, draw a triangle on the paper that measures 2½ inches from the apex to the base, which is 2¾ inches long. It's best to use the natural edge of the paper as your baseline to begin with. Draw a smaller triangle that measures 1 inch from the apex to the base, which is 1-inch wide. Peel the large triangle from the adhesive and center it on a piece of card stock. Center a smaller triangle under it. O Christmas Tree, O Christmas Tree!

Homemade Card Basics

- Before you begin, know the size you want your card to be. Be sure you can buy envelopes to fit the card. When folded, many Christmas cards measure 6¾ inches wide by 5½ inches high. When unfolded, they measure 6¾ inches wide by 10¾ inches high. To design such a card, use a blank piece of 8½- × 11-inch white paper. Cut the width down to about 7¼ inches. Fold it in half and design your cover, interior, and back.

- Know what your nearest copy shop or print shop requires in terms of original design from you and time to produce your card. For example, if you want to use a photograph be sure to check that it will reproduce well on card stock. Discuss your idea with the print shop first, before you spend a lot of time on an idea that proves unworkable.

THE CHRISTMAS TREE

The Christmas tree first came indoors in the seventeenth century, when Germans placed cookies and candles on its branches to represent the life and light of Christ. By the middle of the nineteenth century, the custom had become well rooted in the U.S. Today, the selecting, hauling home, putting up, and trimming of the tree is arguably the most exciting hands-on project in anybody's holiday.

Over a dozen varieties of evergreens are raised on U.S. tree farms specifically for adorning homes at Christmas. My favorites are the fragrant Douglas fir and balsam fir. The Scotch pine and blue spruce are my runner-up choices—the former because its bushy branches, although not so fragrant, add a plump charm to the living room; and its needles are so hardy that they don't shed easily even if they become dry; the latter I love just for its thick and elegant branches.

Making Your Selection

Before you head out to the tree lot or tree farm, make sure you have an idea of what height and width tree you need. If you're heading to the farm, find out if you need your own saw.

It's always best to buy early, when you are bound to get the most perfect tree. The trees first show up in my neighborhood about the first week of December. My contributor, Sharon Kopenski, buys her tree by December 5, even though she doesn't put it up until the fifteenth or so. If you can, buy your tree early and keep it watered and protected in an out-of-the way spot until you're ready to put it up.

Test a tree's freshness by running your fingers pressed together down a tip of branch near the top. If the needles do not break or come off in your hand, but rather show resilience, you've got a fresh tree. You might also lift the tree by the center of the trunk and tap the trunk against the ground just to make sure needles do not come tumbling off.

Care for Your Tree

When you get the tree home, saw off about ½ inch at the bottom of the trunk. This removes the hardened sap coating that the tree formed after it was cut. Stand the tree in a bucket of water. It hasn't had a drink in some days or weeks, so it will take in a gallon or more of water within a few hours and probably a quart a day thereafter. Then place the tree in a cool place, where it is protected from wind and direct sun (a garage or cool room), until the day when you will bring it in for decorating.

Before you bring the tree inside, make sure that your tree stand will fit the trunk of the tree. Also make sure that the stand has a deep water reservoir, not a shallow one. The bigger the reservoir, the less often you will have to water the tree. Then bring the tree in, place it in the stand away from any heat source, and fill the reservoir with water.

To keep the tree fresh and fragrant, check the water level in the stand reservoir every day. Don't let the water level slip below the bottom of the trunk. This can be difficult to accomplish, what with the tree skirt and presents under the tree. To add water, try using a long-necked funnel available in auto parts and hardware stores. Some home decorating stores, such as The Home Depot, offer reasonably priced, state-of-the-art Christmas tree watering devices.

Lights

In my experience, it takes about 200 small multicolored or white lights and about 150 ornaments to adequately deck out an approximately 6-foot tall by 4½-foot wide Christ-

mas tree. Use 100 small lights and 75 ornaments for a
4-foot tall by 3½-foot wide tree.

If you prefer the large old-fashioned red, green, and
gold lights (my favorites), use a little less than half as
many of the small lights required. A 6-foot tree will need
about 85 large lights, and a 4-foot tree about 45.

Check your lights a couple of weeks before you plan
to light your tree. Replace any burned-out bulbs, and buy
new lights to replenish the old strands.

Garlands and Strings

Once the lights are on, it's time to add strings of popcorn
or cranberries or any other garland. You'll need about 70
feet to wrap a 6-foot tree from top to bottom and about
40 feet for a 4-foot tree.

Ornaments

I have discovered that often-used ornaments either matter
deeply to their owners, each carrying a tender signifi-
cance and memory, or they don't matter much at all—
whatever adds sparkle, color and texture is fine. Take your
ornaments out from storage several weeks before Christmas and decide if you want to make or buy new ones, or
do something totally different for a change.

My mother went through a snowy-tree stage for a
few Christmases while I was growing up. Our yearly
Douglas fir, which was usually decorated with large lights,
colored glass balls, and tinsel, was replaced one year by a
blue spruce, with branches sprayed white with fake snow
and decorated with bright red balls.

The next year, the tree was again white but had only

blue ornaments. An electrically rotating color-wheel lamp sat on the floor next to the tree, casting waves of changing colors onto the tree.

After one or two more years of snow-tinged trees bedecked with white lights and bows only or bird ornaments only, we all realized that Mom was trying to create a white Christmas in our Southern California living room. Soon after my family started going to a cabin in the mountains for Christmas.

There, with snow cascading outside, we enjoyed once again a green Douglas fir, warmly lit with reds, greens, and golds and decorated with a cheerful hodgepodge of ornaments and silver tinsel.

Theme Trees

You might want to change the look and feel of your tree this year. Give flight to your creative longings! Here are a few theme suggestions to spark your imagination.

Antique or Victorian Theme

Use small multicolored or gold lights, and garlands of pearls and glass beads. Using a glue gun and ornament hooks or gold thread, hang tiny bells, antique angels, bouquets of dried baby roses, miniature toy drums and stuffed bears, lace hearts, sachets, Victorian Santas cut from Christmas cards, tin toys, and miniature red, white and blue flags or bunting.

❧

Animal Theme

Make gingerbread ducks and pigs and cows. (See Gingerbread recipe, p. 135.) Hang them along with toy horses sprayed gold, papier-mâché doves, ceramic cats, tiny stuffed dinosaurs, photos of family pets, and colored glass ornaments shaped like bears, camels, elephants, and toads.

❧

Toy Theme

Deck your tree with train cabooses, whistles, tiny trumpets and harmonicas, small dolls, tin houses, airplanes, boats and clowns, and garlands of popcorn and ribbons.

❧

Memory Theme

If you have saved everything from over the years, you might have fun making a memorabilia tree. Use your usual lights and many of your old ornaments as a base design, then add small items from you and your family's past that will have meaning: small lightweight framed photographs of you when you were a child, or of your children when they were smaller. Cut and glue portions of photos to ball ornaments. Hang ribbons and medals won at school sports competitions. Tie baby's first shoe to a pink ribbon, the tag from a fondly remembered family dog to a string of gold beads. Hang up some dried flowers from a special bouquet, a matchbook cover from a wedding, I.D. tags from a tour of duty, toys that were once loved; an alphabet block, an egg of silly putty; small crafts made at camp.

Children might enjoy decorating smaller tabletop theme trees by themselves. The theme might be dogs only, birds only, toys, or small drawings.

The Earth Angel Ornament

One year I chose to cover the tree with angels, any kind of angels. If it had wings, it was welcome. In addition to numerous carved wooden angels, ceramic angels with chimes, tubby little stuffed angels, and elegant papier-mâché ones, there were flying pig angels and Earth Angels. My neighbor Barbara McTiernan told me how to make Earth Angels from flora collected in the park near our homes. Because of the different size pinecones used, each one was delightfully different. If your surroundings don't yield all the needed items, your local florist supply store will have what you need.

1 pinecone (any size) brushed clean of surface dirt
1 large acorn, cap still attached, wiped clean
1 whole milkweed pod, opened and dried
1 pipe cleaner
1 golf tee
12-inch length gold thread
Gold spray paint
Glue gun

Hold the pinecone stemside up. This is the body of your angel. Using a glue gun, attach the acorn to the stem of the pinecone. This is the angel's head. Give it a good look over and decide on the best place to attach the milkweed pod wings. Then, using a glue gun, attach the wings to the back of the angel.

The pipe cleaner creates the angel's arms. Wrap it around from the back to front, tucking it under the petals of the pinecone so that the two ends can be shaped as arms. Between the two ends of the pipe cleaner "hands," use the glue gun to affix the golf tee, which is the angel's trumpet. Whether the trumpet is up in the playing position or down in the relaxed position is up to you. Attach the gold thread around the body for hanging. Hang the angel in a spray box and spray with gold paint. Let dry.

A spray box (any large cardboard box at least 2 feet deep) allows you to spray-paint ornaments and decorations in a contained space. Lay the box on its side and cut a small hole in the top. Pull the thread that holds the ornament up through the hole and loop it around a thin stick so that the ornament hangs freely inside the box. Spray the ornament lightly, turning it until it is completely painted. Not all ornaments need to hang in a spray box; some can just sit on the bottom and be turned by hand.

Angel Cut-out Ornaments

I save any card with an angel on it, especially those with Valentine or Christmas angels. These make wonderful ornaments and charming additions to any package wrap. To hang the angel cut-out so that it won't spin on its thread and reveal its undecorated back, you will need pliable glue or a glue gun and some ornament hooks, both available at any craft store or floral supply store.

Angel cut from card
Glue or glue gun
Ornament hook

On the back of the angel at the top, press a BB-size amount of glue. Then press the bottom part of an ornament hook into the glue. Let dry, then hang.

From-the-Oven Ornaments: Gingerbread Stars, Critters, and Things

One of my favorite things to do is to bake new ornaments each year. The hankering must come from my German ancestors, who actually adorned their trees with sweetcakes and cookies.

These ornaments are a snap to make. They can be baked, cooled, wrapped, and frozen long before the tree arrives. Once thawed, you can leave them plain and rustic or ice and decorate them.

Choose simple cookie cutters, 3 inches to 6 inches in size, in any shape you like. Stars and moons can be iced pearly white and sprinkled with gold or silver dragees; animals can be iced or left plain; toys such as cars and planes can be iced and coated with colorful sugar sprinkles; classic gingerbread people, Christmas trees, snowmen, Santas, and Rudolphs also can be iced in the appropriate colors, with licorice dots and Red Hots used for eyes and noses.

If you can't find a cutter for a shape you'd like, draw the shape on lightweight cardboard and cut it out to make your own template. Lay the template on the rolled-out cookie dough and cut around the outline with a sharp knife. Don't use just one size. Ornaments of different sizes and shapes delight the eye.

FOR THE GINGERBREAD DOUGH:
7 cups all-purpose flour
1 teaspoon baking soda
1 1/2 teaspoons salt
2 tablespoons ground ginger
4 teaspoons ground cinnamon
2 teaspoons ground cloves
1 teaspoon ground allspice
1 1/2 cups (3 sticks) unsalted butter, softened
2 cups sugar
2 large eggs, lightly beaten
1 1/2 cups unsulfured molasses

Combine the flour, baking soda, ginger, cinnamon, cloves, and allspice in a large bowl.

In another mixing bowl, or in the bowl of an electric mixer, beat the butter and sugar until light and fluffy. Beat in the eggs and molasses until well combined. Add the flour mixture, and beat well until dough forms. Divide the dough in half and shape each half into a ball; flatten slightly and wrap in plastic wrap. Chill at least 1 hour or keep refrigerated up to 3 days.

Heat the oven to 350°F. Grease one or two cookie sheets. On a well-floured surface, roll out half the dough to about 1/8-inch thickness. Using cookie cutters or templates, cut the dough into desired shapes and place on the prepared cookie sheets. Bake until cookies are firm to the touch, 10 to 12 minutes. Do not let them become too dark around the edges.

Remove the cookies from the oven and, using a wooden skewer or match stick, make a hole in each one about ½ inch from the top. Cool cookies completely on a wire rack before storing or decorating.

MAKES ABOUT 12 3-INCH ORNAMENTS AND 6 6-INCH ORNAMENTS; OR 24 3-INCH ORNAMENTS; OR 12 6-INCH ORNAMENTS.

ROYAL ICING
2 large egg whites
4 cups (about 1 pound) confectioner's sugar
1 tablespoon lemon juice

Combine all ingredients in a large mixing bowl or in the bowl of an electric mixer. Beat until creamy stiff and soft peaks form. If icing is too thick, add a little more lemon juice.

Note: For colored icings, tint small bowls of Royal Icing with food color dyes.

MAKES ABOUT 2½ CUPS.

TO DECORATE:
Silver and gold dragees
Cinnamon Red Hots
Multicolored sugar sprinkles
Licorice strings
Gum drops
Green and red food dye (for coloring the icing)

Place the decorations in the wells of an empty Styrofoam egg carton.

Decorate the cookies one at a time, spreading each with a thin layer of Royal Icing and adding any of the decorating ingredients. Set aside to dry completely.

Some cookies look wonderful without icing or decorating.

Hang the ornaments using colored thread, thin ribbons, or ornament hooks.

THE WREATH

Probably as classic a symbol of Christmas as the tree itself, the wreath is frequently the first thing you see as you cross any threshold during December. It conveys welcome. Being a perfect circle, a wreath is also a symbol of never-ending strength and love, a comforting reminder in the dark days of approaching winter.

The Classic Wreath

A fresh evergreen circular wreath about 26 inches in diameter, decorated with a large bow and several pinecones or small gilded balls or sprigs of millinery fruit and faux berries, is the wreath most of us cherish seeing during the season.

Several large boughs of fresh fir or Scotch pine separated into 3-inch to 6-inch sprigs (Some people prefer to cut their own juniper branches and separate them into sprigs.)

Florist's wire

1 wire wreath form, about 22 inches in diameter for a 26-inch finished wreath

1 large wire-ribbon bow

Assorted small balls with floral wire attached, pinecones, and/or ornaments (Adding a favorite ornament makes a wreath even more memorable.)

Cover a work space or tabletop with newspaper to make clean-up easy.

Make small bunches of the sprigs and wrap the base of the stems tightly with florist's wire, making a bouquet. The fuller the bunches, the fuller your wreath will be. Attach one bunch at a time to the wreath form, using additional florist's wire. Overlap the next bunch so that the greens cover the stems of the previous bouquet. Continue until the form is covered with greens. Affix large bow, bunch of pinecones, or millinery fruit over the place where you last attached a sprig. Leave the wreath simple or add a few more pieces of decoration.

For variations: Mix several different varieties of fresh greens: pine, fir, cypress, and juniper.

The Advent Wreath

A long-established custom in Germany and many Eastern European countries, the Advent Wreath sits on a table in the household throughout December. On each of the four Sundays before Christmas, a red candle is lit and added to the wreath, usually at or just before dinner. By the fourth Sunday four candles are burning in the center of the wreath.

Several large boughs of fresh fir or Scotch pine separated into
    3-inch to 6-inch sprigs
Florist's wire
1 wire wreath form, about 16 to 18 inches in diameter
4 red candles

To make your own Advent Wreath, simply follow the directions for the Classic Wreath but omit decorations, as the Advent Wreath is usually just greens and the red candles.

Theme Wreath: Buy ready-made dried grapevine wreaths, or Styrofoam wreath forms and some bags of peat moss, florist's wire, and wooden pegs at a florist supply or home decoration store, and decorate them according to theme. For a *nature wreath*, you might cover a Styrofoam form with peat moss and wire bunches of pinecones, acorns, red faux berries, dried hydrangeas, and a green bow to wooden pegs and stick them into the wreath. A grapevine wreath and a glue gun is all you need to make a wreath of pinecones, berries, and bows.

Make a Christmas *nut wreath* by using a glue gun to affix walnuts, filberts, and almonds in their shells to a vine wreath or a Styrofoam wreath form; leave it natural or spray it with clear lacquer or even gold paint. When it dries, attach a grosgrain ribbon bow for color.

PROJECTS ESPECIALLY FOR KIDS

As excited young children become impatient about the slow passage of time—when Christmas is so close but also so far away—letting them help make ornaments and greeting cards and trim the tree provides much-needed focus and joy. But as any of us can remember, calming down enough to go to sleep at night was one of the hardest things to do in the Christmas season. Here are some projects that may help end the day.

Growing Santa's Beard

Santa starts out without a beard. The beard grows slowly over the month. When it's full, it's Christmas.

On a large (approximately 9- × 15-inch) piece of heavy poster paper or construction paper, draw Santa's head—hat, eyes, cheeks and smile but just a light-line outline for his beard. Or buy a large Santa face at your local party supply store and carefully cut his beard off and glue him without beard to the poster paper. Add a light-line outline for his beard and hang the beardless Santa inside your child's bedroom door. Every night let your child glue three or four cotton balls into Santa's beard before going to sleep. It takes about 90 cotton balls for a full beard, so to figure how many cotton balls your child can glue on each day, divide 90 by the number of days left until Christmas. If you start Santa's beard on December 5, add 4 balls every night; on December 15, add 9 balls every night.

The Arrival of Rudolph

Rudolph the Red-Nose Reindeer starts out in puzzle pieces. When he's all assembled, complete with his red nose, Christmas is here!

Purchase a large poster of Rudolph the Red-Nose Reindeer at your local party supply store. Trace its outline on a large piece of poster paper or construction paper and hang the outline inside your child's bedroom door. Cut the poster of Rudolph into several pieces—antlers, shoulders, legs, tail, and so on—to be assembled over time. Cut as many pieces as the number of days left until Christmas. Place the pieces, except the nose, in a bag. Each night before going to sleep, your child removes a piece from the bag, finds where it belongs on the outline, and glues it (using a glue stick) on. Save the nose for last.

Going to Bethlehem

If you own a nativity scene, instead of putting it up all at once, do it with your children one piece at a time. First, either read the story of the nativity from the New Testament in St. Luke's Gospel, or tell the story yourself. Describe how Mary and Joseph traveled to Bethlehem and how Christ was born in the stable, how the angels sang and the shepherds came running to see what was happening, and how later the three kings came visiting, too.

Count the pieces in your nativity scene, and start this project that number of days before Christmas. Mary and Joseph count as one piece on December 24 and the infant Jesus is added to the manger on Christmas morning.

If you don't have a nativity scene, each night the children can draw a different piece: first the stable, trees and hills; then the animals that live in the stable—camels, cows, sheep, goats, chickens, ducks, horses, donkeys. As Christmas draws closer, they can start drawing the other people in the Christmas story—shepherds (men, women, children) and their dogs, and the shepherds' families who live nearby. Then they can draw the star in the night sky and all the angels singing, and finally Mary, Joseph, and the infant Jesus in the manger.

Try to limit the size of each drawing so that you can create a somewhat realistic scene in which Mary or Joseph aren't bigger than the camel, for example. When each drawing is finished, use a glue stick to glue it to light-weight cardboard. Then, using good scissors or an X-acto knife, cut out the drawing. Glue another small piece of cardboard to the back so that the piece stands up on its own, creating a three-dimensional scene on a tabletop. Or you can tape the finished piece to a large poster for a two-dimensional nativity scene.

My favorite place for the homemade nativity scene, however, is on the refrigerator. In a craft or electrical supply store, purchase several small magnets. Affix a mag-net to each mounted drawing with a glue gun, and place the drawing on the refrigerator.

Remember, Mary and Joseph arrive next to last and the infant Jesus is last. Merry Christmas!

Checklist for a Handmade Christmas

November 1–7
☆ Decide if you will decorate your tree in a new way this year, make and/or bake new ornaments to add to your collection (and if so, how many), make wreaths to have or to give away, make your own greeting cards, make floral arrangements or centerpieces for gifts.

☆ Collect pinecones, acorns, and flowers for including in homemade gifts.

☆ Shop for materials for homemade crafts and gifts. Begin making them if you've planned on making a lot.

❋

November 8–14
☆ Work on craft projects. (See pp. 128–138.)

☆ Plan and design homemade greeting cards. (See p. 121.)

❋

November 15–21
☆ Check out boxes of old ornaments and decorations; buy any to replenish what you have.

☆ Work on craft projects.

❋

December 1–7
☆ Make an Advent Wreath and place it in a central location. (See p. 140.)

☆ Buy your Christmas tree. (See p. 125.)

☆ Make a wreath to hang on front door or in foyer.

☆ Complete craft projects.

☆ Bake gingerbread ornaments; wrap and freeze for later use. (See p. 135.)

December 8–14

☆   Decorate gingerbread ornaments.

☆   Trim the tree.

CHAPTER IX
Christmas Parties

Having good friends over before Christmas is a pleasurable remedy for the holiday-rush jitters that invariably hit by mid-December. Parties provide a welcome time out from mounting tensions, for lighthearted conversation and genuine expressions of love and friendship.

Christmas parties can be as simple as last-minute casual gatherings where pizza is ordered in and everyone sings carols; as complicated as elegant sit-down dinners by candlelight; and as fun as large informal buffets where Santa might just make an appearance. Some are work parties, too, where Christmas preparations are completed.

At ornament parties, the host supplies simple materials and ideas for easy-to-make ornaments and a buffet of good food and drink. All guests hang a freshly made ornament on the tree but can make as many as they want for their own tree.

Some parents host tree-trimming parties just for the kids and their friends. Each child invites a friend or two for supper. The menu is very simple: soup, pizza, salad, or chili and cornbread. Then it's to the tree, which is already strung with lights. The garlands, ornaments, and tinsel are laid out. Smaller children decorate the low branches; taller children, the high branches. Hot chocolate should be available during the trimming, and Christmas cookies for dessert. Each guest goes home with a gift bag of cookies.

Sharon Kopenski hosts at least two parties before Christmas. One is a sit-down meal for eight or so of her close friends, usually during the third week of December. It's an elegant dinner party that calls for her best china and candlelight in a dining room decked with boughs of fresh pine, flowers, and garlands. Sharon serves simple but memorable food—her favorite menu features seafood-stuffed chicken breast and an out-of-this-world vegetable tart.

After dinner, everyone adjourns to the living room for cheesecake and coffee. Sharon conducts the traditional grab-bag gift exchange. Taking turns, each person reaches into a bag of gifts, chooses one, and opens it.

Sharon's other party traditionally takes place the weekend before Christmas and is a testimony to goodwill, friendship, and the health of nontraditional families. Sharon is a divorcée and has been sharing her life for some time now with her significant other, Al Buss. On the weekend before Christmas, she and Al host a buffet and gift exchange for all of Al's family—his grown children, their significant others, even Al's ex-wife. Sharon says it's a fantastic gathering full of harmony and good spirit.

The buffet is easy but ample; there may be one appetizer—for example, a colorful crudite of carrots, broccoli, cherry tomatoes, and a yogurt/dill dip—beer-baked ham and biscuits, Waldorf salad, mashed sweet potatoes, green bean salad, and, for dessert, vanilla cream pies from Al's ex-wife. Afterward, the exchange of gifts is noisy, even downright raucous, as everybody opens them all at once.

My neighbors Barbara and Charlie McTiernan host their biggest party of the year on Christmas Eve, when they welcome and celebrate friendship with 150 guests. They started this tradition eighteen years ago, when Barbara hosted an intimate dinner party for the three other couples in her baby-sitting pool.

From those three couples, the guest list has grown. Now the parents, relatives, and grown-up children of those original couples; new neighbors and their children; and other McTiernan relatives come.

The McTiernans' house is a perfect setting for just such a homecoming. The large, four-story, Victorian brownstone in Brooklyn, New York, radiates classic charm when it's all "done up" for Christmas. Yards and yards of garland trim the ornate wooden banisters and two polished mantels in the dining and living rooms. Handmade ornaments, collected over the years, decorate the tree, which fills the 14-foot front window. All the artwork that ordinarily graces the walls and staircases has been replaced for the month of December with angels and holly-trimmed sconces holding tall candles, wreaths, ribbons, and pine swags. The wooded foyer is bedecked with pine boughs and fresh flowers.

By the time the first guests ring the bell in the late afternoon, a long, richly decorated buffet table, laden with delicacies, stretches the length of the dining room. Barbara admits that it was difficult to give up the fine china and silver of her first party. Today guests eat from paper (albeit very nice) plates with paper napkins, but, she's happy to say, real cutlery.

Guests help themselves to an ample buffet of hot appetizers—stuffed mushrooms, quiche, and the kids' favorite, sausage in crescent rolls, cool pâtés, tapinade, and creamy cheese spread on crispy baguettes. Later comes bowls of pasta with salmon and capers, or perhaps grilled London broil, tossed vegetable salad in vinaigrette, and finally lots of desserts. Only recently has Barbara begun to allow guests to bring anything. If they insist, she requests Christmas cookies.

For the little children who don't like the grown-up food or who are too much in a hurry to wait to eat, there's a six-foot hero sandwich all cut and ready for little hands to help themselves in the family room downstairs. For the kids, too, an entire corner of the living room is set up with wooden toys, some quite old but still indestructible. There are movable fantasy farms and village buildings, animals, cars and trucks, street scenes with tin policemen. There's a basket of ornaments that didn't make it to the tree, and some kids make Christmas over and over in the corner full of toys.

Music streams through the entire house, as does non-stop conversation. And there's always a game of football in the street out front.

The gathering is usually over by 8:00 P.M. or so, allowing everyone time for Christmas Eve with their own families. Last year, however, dozens of folk stayed late, carrying the McTiernans' party on until past 10:00.

❦ ❦ ❦

SOME BUFFET TRADITIONS

Classic Eggnog

This creamy-rich and spirited drink dates back at least to 1775 America, when Christmas cooks would beat eggs with cream, sugar, and rum, whiskey, or brandy and serve it to revelers. In the old days, a cook whipped this up quickly in a mixing bowl, chilled it, and served. Nowadays, because of the possibility of Salmonella poisoning from eating raw eggs, it's best to cook the egg mixture before chilling it.

6 eggs, beaten
2 cups milk
1/2 cup plus 2 tablespoons sugar
2 tablespoons light rum
2 tablespoons brandy
1 teaspoon vanilla
1 cup whipping cream
Freshly ground nutmeg

In a medium saucepan, combine the eggs, milk, 1/2 cup sugar, and cook, stirring, over medium heat until mixture thickens enough to coat a metal spoon. Remove from heat and cool slightly. Stir in rum, brandy, and vanilla, and chill at least 4 hours.

To serve, whip the heavy cream with the 2 tablespoons sugar in a large bowl until stiff peaks form. Transfer chilled eggnog to a punch bowl and fold in all but ½ cup of the whipped cream. Ladle the eggnog into serving glasses and top with reserved whipped cream and a pinch of nutmeg.

MAKES 10 4-OUNCE SERVINGS.

Brazilian Coffee Nog

This eggnog variation is delicious hot or cold, and is an excellent choice for a holiday brunch.

1 cup milk
1 cup light cream
2 eggs, separated
2 tablespoons sugar
2 cups brewed strong espresso coffee
¼ cup coffee-flavored liqueur (optional)
1 cup heavy or whipping cream
Ground cinnamon
2 teaspoons grated orange zest

In a medium saucepan, combine the milk, light cream, egg yolks, and sugar and cook, stirring, over medium heat until mixture thickens and coats a metal spoon. Remove from heat and stir in the coffee and liqueur, if desired. Chill for at least 4 or up to 24 hours.

To serve, beat the egg whites in a bowl until stiff but not dry. Fold whites into the chilled eggnog and transfer to a punch bowl. Beat the cream in a large bowl until soft peaks form. Ladle the eggnog into serving glasses. Top each with whipped cream, a dash of cinnamon, and a sprinkling of orange zest.

Note: To serve warm, simply serve after cooking, eliminating the egg whites.

MAKES **14** 4-OUNCE SERVINGS.

Beer-Baked Bourbon-Glazed Ham

Sharon Kopenski likes to serve this at informal buffet parties. I can understand why. The slow-baked spirit-glazing make this ham meltingly tender and moist. Serve it along with Mashed Sweet Potatoes, green beans, classic Waldorf Salad (recipe follows), and biscuits.

15-pound precooked ham with bone
1 pound (1 box) plus 2 cups dark brown sugar
8 12-ounce containers beer
1/4 cup honey
1/4 cup Dijon-style mustard
1/2 cup bourbon

Preheat the oven to 325°F. Place the ham in a roasting pan. Sprinkle with 1 pound of the sugar, patting firmly until the ham is completely coated on all sides. Pour the beer into the pan and bake, covered, 3¾ hours.

One hour before done, pour off all but ½ inch of liquid in pan. In a small saucepan combine the honey, mustard, 2 cups sugar, and bourbon. Cook over medium heat until sugar is dissolved. Baste ham every 10 minutes for remaining 1 hour with pan juices and honey-bourbon glaze.

Cool slightly and slice.

SERVES 10 TO 12.

Mashed Sweet Potatoes

These taste great hot or at room temperature and make a perfect accompaniment for Beer-Baked Bourbon-Glazed Ham.

10 *large sweet potatoes*
8 *tablespoons (1 stick) butter, softened*
1/2 *cup milk or light cream, warmed*
3 *tablespoons maple syrup*
Salt and freshly ground pepper

In a large pot, boil the potatoes in their jackets until tender, about 45 minutes. Drain and cool slightly.

Peel the potatoes and return them to the pot. Mash the potatoes until smooth. Stir in the butter, cream, and maple syrup. Add salt and pepper to taste.

SERVES 12.

Traditional Waldorf Salad

This salad has appeared so often at my family holiday buffets that I had to include it. Yes, it *was* invented by Chef Oscar of the Waldorf-Astoria in New York City in 1893.

2 cups diced celery
2 cups diced peeled apples
1 cup chopped walnuts
1¼ cups low-fat mayonnaise

In a large mixing bowl, combine the celery, apples, and walnuts. Add the mayonnaise and toss until well coated. Cover and chill or serve immediately.

SERVES 12.

Tom Folan's Grilled Cornish Hens with Spicy Rice

Grilled game hens are a Christmas Eve sit-down-dinner tradition in the Folan household. Tom Folan slow-cooks the birds on a covered grill over oakwood smoke heat. You'll need a drip pan (any shallow aluminum or foil pan). If you aren't lucky enough to have California-style outdoor grilling weather, roast these hens in the oven at 350°F.

Make the dressing ahead (even a day ahead) and warm it through before serving. Serve with glazed carrots, fresh green salad, hot rolls, and chocolate cake or cream puffs for dessert.

FOR THE DRESSING
3 fresh chorizo (Spanish sausage)
1 tablespoon unsalted butter or margarine
1 medium onion, chopped
1 clove garlic, minced
1/2 cup diced green or red bell pepper
1 cup chopped, seeded peeled tomatoes
1/4 teaspoon sugar
1/4 cup chicken stock
2 tablespoons chopped fresh cilantro
1/2 teaspoon freshly grated orange zest
1/4 teaspoon chili powder
1/2 cup chopped cooked ham
2 1/4 cups cooked rice
Salt and freshly ground black pepper

Heat the olive oil in a heavy skillet over medium heat. Add the sausages and cook until well browned on all sides, about 8 minutes. Drain on paper towels and cut into ¼-inch thick slices. Set aside.

Heat the butter in a large skillet over medium heat. Add the onion and garlic and cook until tender and golden, about 5 minutes. Add the bell peppers; cook 2 minutes. Add the tomatoes, sugar, stock, cilantro, orange zest, and chili powder, and cook 3 minutes. Stir in the ham and cook 2 minutes.

Transfer to a large bowl and add the reserved sausages and the rice. Add salt and pepper to taste. Spoon mixture into a baking dish. Cover tightly and place in a warm oven until ready.

FOR THE HENS
6 fresh Cornish game hens
⅓ cup olive oil
2 cloves garlic, finely minced
1 teaspoon freshly chopped rosemary
2 tablespoons freshly squeezed lemon juice

Wash the hens and wipe them dry inside and out. Combine the olive oil, garlic, rosemary, and lemon juice in a small bowl and stir until well blended. Brush this mixture over the hens; cover loosely and let stand 30 minutes. Reserve remaining marinade.

Prepare the coals and preheat the grill. Bank the hot coals to one end of the coal grate and place a drip pan at the other end. Sprinkle presoaked oakwood chips over the hot coals. Brush the grid with oil. Place the hens on the grid, over the drip pan, breast side up.

Cook, covered, over medium-hot heat with the vents half open for 15 minutes. Baste with drippings and continue to cook, basting every 15 minutes until juices run yellow when hen is pierced with a fork.

SERVES 6.

Sharon Kopenski's Shrimp-Stuffed Chicken Breasts

Sharon Kopenski's elegant Christmas party dinner might begin with a pumpkin soup, followed by these delicious stuffed chicken breasts served with wild rice, steamed broccoli, and an irresistible vegetable tart (recipe follows). For dessert: chocolate trifle. Save time and ask your butcher to skin and bone the poultry.

4 large chicken breasts, halved, skinned, boned
¼ cup unsalted butter or margarine
⅓ cup sliced green onions
1 pound mushrooms, cleaned and sliced
3 tablespoons flour
Salt and white pepper
½ teaspoon dried thyme
¾ cup chicken stock
½ cup milk
⅓ cup dry white wine
1 cup shredded Gruyère Cheese
6 ounces small shrimp, shelled and deveined
2 tablespoons minced parsley
⅓ dry bread crumbs
½ cup sliced almonds

Preheat the oven to 375°F. Lightly butter a 9- × 13-inch baking dish. Pound the chicken breasts between waxed paper with a wooden mallet until 1/4-inch thick. Set aside.

Heat the butter in a large skillet over medium heat. Add the onions and mushrooms and cook until tender, about 6 minutes. Sprinkle the mixture with the flour, salt, and pepper, and stir until well combined. Add the thyme, stock, milk, and wine, and cook, stirring, over medium heat, until sauce is smooth. Stir in half the cheese and continue cooking until thickened.

In a small bowl combine the shrimp, parsley, and bread crumbs. Stir in 1/4 cup of the sauce, mixing until well combined. Divide shrimp mixture into 8 equal portions. Place each portion in the center of each chicken breast. Roll the meat around the stuffing and place, seam side down, in the prepared dish. Pour remaining sauce over the rolled chicken. Bake 20 minutes. Sprinkle with remaining cheese and sliced almonds and bake 5 minutes more, until cheese is melted and almonds are brown.

SERVES 8.

Festive Vegetable Tart

This special-occasion dish is a wonderful addition to any buffet or dinner table. It requires a lot of preparation, but much of it can be done ahead of time. Sharon chops the vegetables the day before and stores them in zip-lock bags. When using the phyllo dough, be sure to work quickly and keep any remaining dough covered with a wet towel, as phyllo dries out quickly.

1 10-ounce box chopped frozen spinach, thawed, squeezed dry

2 tablespoons fresh rosemary or 1 tablespoon dried

1 small onion, minced

2 cloves garlic, minced

1/2 cup feta cheese, crumbled

1/4 cup skim milk

1/2 teaspoon salt

1/2 teaspoon fresh ground black pepper

1/2 teaspoon olive oil

1/4 cup dry white wine

2 medium zucchini, sliced 1/8-inch thick on the diagonal

1 medium onion, peeled, sliced, and separated into rings

1/2 pound mushrooms, sliced

1/2 teaspoon olive oil

1/2 pound frozen phyllo dough, thawed

4 red bell peppers, roasted, cut into long strips

7-ounce jar marinated artichoke hearts, drained and chopped

1 3-ounce bag sun-dried tomatoes, reconstituted and cut into slivers

2 tablespoons slivered fresh basil leaves

1/2 cup toasted pine nuts

Preheat the oven to 375°F.

In the container of a food processor, combine the spinach, rosemary, onion, garlic, feta, milk, salt and pepper, and process until smooth. Set aside.

In a large nonstick skillet, heat the olive oil over medium heat. Add the wine and heat until simmering. Add the zucchini and cook until tender, about 5 minutes. Remove the zucchini and drain on paper towels. Add the onions to the skillet and cook until tender, 5 minutes. Remove and drain on paper towels. Add the mushrooms to the skillet and cook until tender, 5 minutes. Remove and drain on paper towels.

Brush a 10-inch pie plate with oil. Line the pan with phyllo dough by laying down one sheet at a time, brushing each lightly with oil as you go. For edges of dough that extend beyond the pan, crinkle the edges and brush with oil. Do this until all the dough is used.

Spread the spinach puree mixture over bottom of phyllo crust. Arrange the zucchini, onion, mushrooms, roasted peppers, artichoke hearts, and sun-dried tomatoes in layers over the spinach mixture. Bake 15 minutes or until phyllo is golden and crisp and vegetables are warmed through.

Sprinkle with basil and pine nuts. Cut into slices and serve immediately.

SERVES 6 TO 8.

Barbara McTiernan's Yule Log

Here is a rolled chocolate-rich cake that makes a grand entrance and performs a fast disappearing act at the McTiernans' Christmas buffet. Try it for your buffet, too.

FOR THE YULE LOG CAKE

6 ounces chocolate morsels

1 teaspoon instant coffee

3 teaspoons water

5 eggs, separated

1 1/4 cups sugar

1 teaspoon vanilla

1 quart vanilla ice cream, softened

1 quart raspberry or orange sherbet, softened

Heat the oven to 350°F. Lightly grease a 15 1/2-inch × 10 1/2-inch jelly roll pan. Line the bottom with waxed paper; grease and flour the waxed paper.

In the top of a double boiler combine the chocolate morsels, coffee, and water. Melt over hot but not boiling water until smooth. Cool.

In a mixing bowl, beat the egg yolks with 3/4 cup sugar until light and fluffy. Stir in the cooled chocolate and vanilla. In another bowl, beat the whites with 1/2 cup sugar until stiff but not dry. Fold the whites into the chocolate mixture until blended. Pour the batter into the prepared pan and spread evenly.

Bake until the center springs back when pressed with fingertip, 12 to 18 minutes. Cool on a rack.

Spread waxed paper on a countertop and unmold cake onto it. Trim uneven edges of the cake, so all edges are straight. Beginning at the short end of the cake, spread all the ice cream onto about one-third of the cake and carefully roll up the end, leaving about two-thirds of cake empty. Then spread the sherbet on the next third of the cake and continue to roll. With the seam-side down, wrap the roll in waxed paper and place in the freezer.

FOR THE GLAZE
6 ounces semisweet chocolate
2 tablespoons butter or margarine
3 tablespoons milk
2 tablespoons corn syrup
Dark cocoa or confectioner's sugar (optional)

In the top of a double boiler combine the chocolate, butter, milk, and corn syrup. Melt over hot but not boiling water until smooth.

To serve: Unwrap the frozen Yule Log and place it on a serving platter. Drizzle the glaze over the top until the log is well covered and the imperfections and breaks in the cake are disguised. Dust with cocoa or confectioner's sugar, if desired, and decorate the platter with fresh holly or other Christmas greens. Cut the roll into ¾-inch thick slices and serve with fudge sauce, if desired.

SERVES 12 TO 14.

Ginny Folan's Christmas Brunch Casserole

Ginny makes this a couple of weeks before Christmas, covers it tightly, and freezes it. She takes it out to thaw the night before Christmas brunch. The next day, it's ready in 20 minutes.

12 eggs, scrambled
5 medium potatoes, cooked in their jackets, cubed
½ pound bacon, cooked, crumbled
½ cup chopped green onions
2½ cups grated cheddar cheese
Salt and pepper
1 cup salsa (optional)
1 avocado, sliced (optional)
1 cup sour cream (optional)

Heat the oven to 350°F. Layer a 9- × 13-inch pan with one-third each of the eggs, potatoes, bacon, onion, and cheese. Repeat layers, beginning with the eggs and ending with the cheese. Season with salt and pepper to taste.

Bake 15 minutes or until bubbly and heated through.
Serve with salsa and avocado or sour cream if desired.

SERVES UP TO 6.

Sweet Roll Christmas Tree

Baked in the shape of a Christmas tree, these
sweet rolls have delighted the Folan kids for years.
Using 2½-inch biscuit cutters, this recipe makes
two 12-roll trees. Serve this coffee cake for a special brunch or while the presents are being opened
on Christmas morning. It's great to keep on hand
for neighbors who might drop in, too.

1 packet active dry yeast
½ cup warm water (105°–110°F)
¼ cup unsalted butter, melted, plus ¼ cup unsalted butter, softened
¼ cup sugar
¾ cup buttermilk
1 egg, lightly beaten
1 teaspoon baking powder
1 teaspoon salt
3–4 cups all-purpose flour
½ cup brown sugar
¼ cup dark raisins
½ teaspoon cinnamon
Confectioners' Icing (recipe follows)
Candied cherries (optional)

Dissolve the yeast in the water in a large bowl. Let stand for 5 minutes. Add the melted butter, sugar, buttermilk, egg, baking powder, and salt and stir until well combined. Stir in enough of the flour to make a stiff dough. Knead the dough on a lightly floured surface until smooth, about 10 minutes. Place in a lightly oiled bowl. Cover with a damp cloth and place in a warm, draft-free place until doubled in volume, about 1 hour.

Preheat the oven to 350°F. Lightly grease 2 baking sheets.

Punch dough down and roll out on a lightly floured surface into a rectangle 18 × 12 inches. Spread with ¼ cup softened butter; sprinkle with brown sugar, raisins, and cinnamon. With a 2½-inch round cookie cutter, cut out 24 pieces. Arrange 12 pieces on each of the baking sheets to form a Christmas tree. Cover with a damp towel and let rise 30 minutes. Bake 20 minutes or until golden. Allow to cool slightly before icing.

Spread the icing evenly over the tops of the rolls. Decorate with candied cherries if desired.

MAKES 2 CHRISTMAS TREES.

CLASSIC WHITE ICING
2 egg whites
3½ cups confectioner's sugar, sifted
Juice of 1 lemon

In a large bowl, beat the egg whites until stiff but not dry.

Gradually fold in the sugar and lemon juice until it's a good consistency for spreading. If icing is too thick, add more lemon juice.

Checklist for the Perfect Christmas Party

November 7–14
☆   Plan holiday party(ies): date(s), time(s), guest list, and menu ideas.

November 22–30
☆   Mail or telephone with Christmas party invitations.

December 1–7
☆   Plan your party menu; if guests are to bring food, ask for an appetizer that can be served at room temperature, or a hot dish that can be brought and served in its own dish. Guests also can bring Christmas cookies for dessert.

☆   Plan your party decorations. Make sure intended tablecloths fit. For inexpensive, last-minute table coverings, consider buying fabric—plaid, green, or red—and making your own. It's quick and dependable. Also, bright paper cloths from the party goods store look festive under your good lace tablecloth.

December 8–14

☆   Two days before the party, set aside cutlery, serving dishes, serving utensils, plates, napkins, and accessories. Make sure serving utensils are big enough and adequate for people to serve themselves with one hand.

☆   One day before the party, arrange the buffet tables and seating. Put out the linens or napkins, glassware, china or paper plates, and silverware.

☆   On the day of the party:

- Ready your Christmas party atmosphere. Check your sound system, select Christmas tapes and CDs. (See p. 171.) Ask someone in the family to take charge of music during the party. Put flowers, pine arrangements, and candles in holders.
- Slow-simmer some cider and spices in a small pan in the kitchen. It is soothing and lifts the spirit.
- Set up bar and beverages. Ask a family member to take charge of the bar when party gets under way.
- Prepare the buffet table for showing off the food. An exciting and appetizing buffet is one that treats the eyes as well as the mouth. A buffet that offers a variety of colors and textures is appealing. If you don't have chafing dishes on burner racks or cake stands to create height and levels on your buffet, you can create variation by turning one or two colorful empty bowls or dishes upside down and using

them as pedestals for your serving dishes. Or place books right under the tablecloth to create elevation.

Fresh fruit—apples, tangerines, clementines, pears, persimmons, oranges, pomegranates—piled high in a shallow bowl, surrounded by pinecones and faux berries and fresh greens, makes a lovely centerpiece. It will brighten the table as well as disguise the lifts and pedestals.

MUSIC, PLEASE

There's a lot of Christmas music available these days, and it's not just old-fashioned carols sung by a choir, either. In any well-stocked record store, you might find a dozen renditions of "Silent Night" in an array of musical styles—rock, pop, country, jazz, rhythm and blues, symphonic, liturgical . . .

When freshening up your Christmas music collection, buy a little of everything—traditional carols and songs by popular vocalists as well as jazz improvisations, rousing symphonic performances, upbeat instrumentals and mellow renditions of standards by solo instrumental artists. Also, buy Christmas folk music from other countries and cultures—Ireland, Jamaica, South America, Mexico, Germany . . .

For musical atmosphere at your nondancing party, make one or two tapes of a variety of Christmas sounds, as eclectic a mix as you can make it. If your collection is too meager to make an interesting tape, borrow from friends until you have twenty-five or so selections.

Excerpts and cuts from the following would make it onto my party tape, and all are available in the record stores:

The Sinatra Christmas Album by Frank Sinatra

The Nat King Cole Christmas by Nat King Cole

A Charlie Brown Christmas by Vince Guaraldi Trio

Kenny G Miracles by Kenny G

Jazz to the World by various artists

We Wish You a Merry Christmas by John Williams and the Boston Pops

Christmas in the Country, Skitch Henderson and the New York Pops

Merry Mancini by Henry Mancini and Orchestra

Christmas Goes Baroque by various artists

A Jazzy Wonderland by Harry Connick Jr., Winston Marsalis et al

Christmas Guitars by various artists

The Christmas Album by The Canadian Brass

Noel Noel by Leontyne Price with the Montreal Symphony Orchestra

A Very Special Christmas with solos by various rock artists to benefit the Special Olympics

Christmas Greetings from the Vienna Boys Choir by the Vienna Boys Choir

Cabaret Noel by various cabaret singers to benefit Broadway Cares

Save the Children Christmas by Broadway casts to benefit Save the Children Fund

December by George Winston

Winter's Coming Home, Songs to Celebrate Winter and Christmas by the Monks of Western Priory in Weston, Vermont

Glad Tidings by the Choir of the Brooklyn Oratory

Mannheim Steamroller Christmas by Mannheim Steamroller

CHAPTER X

The Circle of Christmas Nights

Christmas Eve to Christmas Night is often called the Circle of Christmas Nights. It is a mysterious time—an extraordinary twenty-four hours that hover apart from ordinary time like a luminescent sphere. It draws us in, lifts us from the anxiety of the past and allows us to linger for a while before we head into the long stretch of winter yet to come.

Once inside the Circle of Christmas Nights, we experience what I call the mystery of Christmas. It has an almost tangible character. If you've ever journeyed out on Christmas Eve, maybe to run an errand or even to catch a plane, or if you've taken a walk on Christmas day or sat looking at the Christmas night sky, you may have felt it. There is a calm in the streets, a quiet focus in others, an absence of apprehension, a general ease and readiness for laughter.

I don't believe this quality descends upon us just because the Christmas rush is over. I believe that for a short while the world around us is truly transformed because hundreds of thousands of people have taken time out to live life differently for one day—to mark the passage of Christmas with shared acts of love, joy, faith, and hope. These acts are the traditions that spring up and thrive year after year in lives of all those who celebrate Christmas.

Reach into memory and find which family customs

and traditions transformed the circle of Christmas nights into a special time at your house.

- On Christmas Eve, perhaps you went caroling in the neighborhood after supper, or made cookies for Santa.
- On Christmas day, your favorite uncle took charge of the annual front-yard snowman contest. When there was no snow, it was a touch football or basketball game.
- At Christmas dinner, your mother placed a lighted candle in the window, to welcome any stranger, who would, she believed, represent Christ.
- Grace before the meal was said by the oldest.
- The wishbone went to the youngest.
- Afterward, your dad started a game of charades—the only time you played all year.

Traditions—those games, stories, songs, prayers and activities that are repeated each year within the Circle of Christmas Nights—help us to experience and share with others the wonderful emotional gifts of Christmas: anticipation, excitement, wonder, joy, comfort, and peace. They help transform an ordinary get-together into a magical, even exuberant event.

What your traditions are doesn't matter; merely having one or two is sufficient. As long as they are simple and have a positive effect on everyone, they will live long. Traditions-to-be can spring to life quite spontaneously and naturally. The impulse to sing "Silent Night" together around the dinner table instead of saying grace could become a well-held tradition, repeated each Christmas Eve. After dinner on Christmas night, the impulse to turn out all the lights except for the Christmas tree lights and listen to Dylan Thomas's recording of "A Child's Christmas in Wales" also could become a family tradition. A desire to take a long walk or bike or car ride after breakfast Christmas morning could become another.

On Christmas Eve, my friends the Folans go to mass with their large extended family. Afterward, Tom Folan prepares his now-celebrated grilled Cornish game hens.

At Nancy Creal's house in Connecticut, her sons get to open one present and then, just before sleep, everybody tells stories or shares memories of Christmases past.

At the McTiernans' in Brooklyn, stockings filled with presents are hung on the bedposts of their now-grown sons, who, just like always, will wake up earlier than everyone, open their gifts, and rouse their parents with laughter and noise.

In California, my cousin Mary Alice Jann and her family drive to the in-laws on Christmas Eve with the car full of kids, gifts, and food, ready to spend the night.

At Sharon Kopenski's house in Wisconsin, all her grown children have arrived back home and everybody pitches in to make an elegant sit-down meal. At each place setting is a candle that appears only on this night, at this meal. Each person lights the candle and makes a wish. In the morning, they will take their time opening their presents.

The Circle of Christmas Nights is rich with possibilities for out-of-the-ordinary acts that could become traditions for you and your loved ones. They needn't be weighty, lengthy, or expensive acts. Something as simple as lighting a candle or singing a song together on Christmas Eve can be very meaningful.

Traditions needn't continue when they're no longer appropriate—when the kids outgrow baking cookies for Santa, for example. When a tradition doesn't allow everybody to experience the best emotions of Christmas, it's time to let it go and start another.

Here are a few suggestions to help you start or to add to your traditions within the Circle of Christmas Nights. Choose one or two special things to do together, night, morning and night.

CHRISTMAS EVE

To make sure you can enjoy the Circle of Christmas Nights, be sure to have packages wrapped and large tasks done so that Christmas Eve can be yours to enjoy.

Have a dinner on Christmas Eve that is simple, pleases your family, and has a special character. If you're planning to have a big Christmas day feast and you don't want to spend time in the kitchen, order pizza or take-out fried chicken for Christmas Eve. If you rarely go out, then go out for dinner. It doesn't matter if this dinner is elaborate or very simple, but let it be ample and full of comfort foods—shepherds' pie, chicken pot pie, pot roast and mashed potatoes, Irish stew, roast chicken and stuffing are all favorites.

Attend Christmas Eve mass or a carol-sing service.

Bring out your Christmas photo albums and share stories from Christmases past.

Bake some refrigerator cookies to welcome Santa.

Watch a video together. *It's a Wonderful Life* with Jimmy Stewart is a terrific experience for anyone over ten years old. Everyone will like *The Muppet Christmas Carol.*

Don't be afraid to create a little drama—turn down the living room lights and read " 'Twas the Night Before Christmas" by candlelight. Or read the story of the birth of Christ from St. Luke's Gospel in the New Testament.

Let your small children place their favorite stuffed animals under the tree or near the chimney or window as a welcoming party for Santa.

After everyone has gone to bed, hang Christmas stockings on bedroom doorknobs or bedposts. When the kids wake up and open the stockings, their laughter and conversation will be your alarm to get up and turn on the tree lights.

Also, after everyone has gone to bed, arrange surprise presents under the tree. Create even more excitement for the morning by hanging white, store-bought papier-mâché birds on bright ribbons from the ceiling circling the tree.

Set up an electric train under or near the tree.

Set up the nativity scene.

With an audio timer (which costs about $10 at your local Radio Shack), set your CD player to play "O Come All Ye Faithful" at the time you want everyone to wake up on Christmas morning. (See "Music, Please," p. 171, for other choices.)

Reminder: Remove preprepared foods from freezer to serve for breakfast.

CHRISTMAS MORNING

Take a before and after photo of everyone around the tree.

Play Christmas music all morning long.

Take all morning to open presents—each person opening theirs while the others watch. Let the youngest or the oldest play Santa and hand out gifts.

Or open all at once with lots of fervor and excitement.

Save one gift each to be opened on Christmas night.

Follow presents with what might become a traditional breakfast. At the Creal house, it's waffles, strawberries and cream. At the Folans, it's a hearty breakfast casserole of eggs and bacon. At the Kopenskis', it's juice and coffee and homemade rolls and coffee cake, while opening presents.

CHRISTMAS DAY

Christmas day could be anything-can-happen time. Young ones might involve themselves with toys and puzzles. Older ones might take a walk, see a movie, go for a bike ride, take a nap. However, be sure to set a time for everyone to get together again, perhaps one hour before the meal to help with preparations and share experiences of the day.

In the Creal house, they start a jigsaw puzzle, leaving it out all day and into the next week until it's finished.

Call relatives and old friends.

CHRISTMAS NIGHT

Start a tradition of inviting someone who would otherwise spend Christmas alone to have dinner with you.

Open the present saved from the morning.

After dessert, or just before bed, gather in the living room, and with everyone lying down or sitting comfortably, play the Dylan Thomas recording of "A Child's Christmas in Wales." The poem takes us into a boy's experience of Christmas day and night and finally his last thoughts before sleep.

ACKNOWLEDGMENTS

Thank you to the dozens of people who contributed Christmas experiences, traditions, time-saving tips, organizational secrets, and favorite recipes. Most special thank-you's go to those contributors whose names appear often in these pages. To my friends in Santa Barbara, California, Ginny and Tom Folan and their sons, Michael and Kevin, thanks for the charming handmade Christmas cards and delicious homemade treats, which each year have kept me grounded in the real joy of the holiday.

Thanks to Sharon Kopenski in Madison, Wisconsin, who entertains enthusiastically during the holidays and whose three grown children return each year for a Christmas homecoming. Her sharing of family traditions was the inspiration for the last chapter.

To my cousin Mary Alice Jann who lives in Visalia, California, with her husband, Jim, and their sons, Jeffrey and Christopher, who loves Christmas because of the opportunity it affords her to hop in the car and connect with family in different parts of the state. Thanks for the many travel tips.

Thanks to Nancy Creal in New Haven, Connecticut, who is a social worker and recently divorced mother of two sons, Jason and David, for reminding me that any celebration of Christmas has to be rooted in treasured memories and traditions.

To my dear friends Phillip Schulz and George Moskowitz, who every year expertly make a warm and sumptuous Christmas dinner for friends and loved ones, thanks for the recipes and organizational tips.

Thanks to my neighbor, Barbara McTiernan in Brooklyn, New York, whose busy life as mother, wife, neighborhood organizer, and fund-raiser includes making preparations for Christmas all year long.

Thanks to Sharon Creal for her shared memories and for patiently helping me construct my first draft, and thanks to my editor, Rob Robertson, who expertly smoothed into final shape this *Checklist for a Perfect Christmas.*

Finally, thanks to my mother, Clara Brown; my brothers, John, Jim, and Gordie; and my dad, Gordon Blahnik, for helping shape my own memories of Christmases.